BREAD OF LIFE,
CUP OF SALVATION

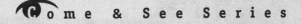
Come & See Series

The **Come & See Series** from Sheed & Ward is modeled on Jesus' compassionate question: "What do you seek?" and his profound invitation to "Come and see" the world through the eyes of faith (John 1:38–39). The series offers spiritual seekers lively, thought-provoking, and accessible books that explore topics of faith and the Catholic Christian tradition. Each book in the series is written by trustworthy guides who are the very best teachers, theologians, and scholars.

Series Editors: James Martin, S.J.
Jeremy Langford

BREAD OF LIFE, CUP OF SALVATION
Understanding the Mass

John F. Baldovin, S.J.

A Sheed & Ward Book

ROWMAN & LITTLEFIELD PUBLISHERS, INC.

Lanham • Boulder • New York • Toronto • Oxford

A SHEED & WARD BOOK

ROWMAN & LITTLEFIELD PUBLISHERS, INC.

Published in the United States of America
by Rowman & Littlefield Publishers, Inc.
A wholly owned subsidary of The Rowman & Littlefield Publishing
Group, Inc.
4501 Forbes Boulevard, Suite 200, Lanham, Maryland 20706
www.rowmanlittlefield.com

PO Box 317
Oxford
OX2 9RU, UK

British Library Cataloguing in Publication Information Available

Library of Congress Cataloging-in-Publication Data

Baldovin, John Francis.
    Bread of life, cup of salvation : understanding the Mass /
John F. Baldovin.
        p. cm. — (Come & see)
    "A Sheed & Ward book."
    Includes bibliographical references and index.
    ISBN 0-7425-3180-5 (alk. paper) — ISBN 0-7425-3179-1
(pbk. : alk. paper)
    1. Mass. I. Title. II. Series.
BX2230.3 .B35 2004
264'.02036—dc22   2003015511

Printed in the United States of America

♾️^TM The paper used in this publication meets the minimum requirements
of American National Standard for Information Sciences—Permanence of
Paper for Printed Library Materials, ANSI/NISO Z39.48-1992.

Dedication

To the People of God at
St. Leo the Great Parish, Oakland, California
St. Paschal Baylon Parish, Oakland, California
Sacred Heart Parish, Lexington, Massachusetts

Contents

Acknowledgments

A book is never simply the product of an author's work. This book is no exception. I want to express my gratitude to those who made it both possible and enjoyable. First of all to my home institution, Weston Jesuit School of Theology, and its president, Robert Manning, S.J., for a year's academic leave that gave me time to do this work. Next I would like to thank the library staffs at Episcopal Divinity School/Weston Jesuit School of Theology Library, Heythrop College, London, and the Pontifical Oriental Institute in Rome. John McDade, S.J., principal of Heythrop College, and Hector Vall Villardell, S.J., rector of the Pontifical Oriental Institute, both offered me hospitality as a visiting scholar. I am very grateful to them as well as to the Farm Street Jesuit Community in London.

This work was vastly improved by the excellent editorial advice of James Martin, S.J., and Jeremy Langford, coeditors of the Come and See series. I am grateful to them.

Finally, I dedicate this book to the people of three parishes where I have had the privilege to preside and preach at the Eucharist over the past twenty years: St. Leo the Great, Oakland, California; St. Paschal Baylon, Oakland, California; and Sacred Heart, Lexington, Massachusetts.

Introduction

I suppose all worshipers can look back on occasions when an experience of the Mass caught them up and drew them out of themselves to recognize the presence and the beauty and the power of God. At least I hope that is the case. I grew up in the 1950s and 1960s, a time of great transition in Catholic liturgy. I can remember very well the Latin Masses of my youth at St. Paul's Church, Clifton, New Jersey. St. Paul's is a beautiful neo-Gothic church built in the 1920s. The building was always very well cared for, and the liturgy showed the same care and attention. I can easily recall being fascinated by the complexity and the holiness of the liturgy celebrated there and—to this day—attribute my interest in the liturgy to those early experiences. With the Second Vatican Council (1962–1965) came a critical moment in the history of the Roman Catholic Church. This council, consisting of every bishop from around the world as well as theological advisers and guests from other Christian churches and the first in almost one hundred years, produced sixteen official documents. The first document to be issued was the *Constitution on the Sacred Liturgy* (December 3, 1963). The Liturgy Constitution initiated a profound reform and renewal of Catholic liturgy, which had been static and unchanging in the previous five hundred years. This came about especially through the adoption of English, the rearrangement of the sanctuary with the priest now facing the assembly across the altar and the readings done from the ambo (lectern), and new forms of music. We Catholics entered into a period of profound change and adaptation, and forty years later we are still learning how to appreciate the power and the meaning of what God is doing for us in the sacrament of the Eucharist. Our experience is showing us that it takes a long time to make the spirit of the liturgy our own.

Some of our liturgies are excellent and moving. Many are not. Experience is beginning to show us that although God is the main "actor" at every Mass, it takes a considerable human effort on our part to respond to God's invitation. Although much of what happens in the liturgy is the responsibility of our clergy and other liturgical ministers, this book is not so much about what *they* do as it is about our appreciation of the Eucharist as we celebrate it today.

The number of books that have been written on the liturgy of the Mass and its theology would fill a large library. So why add another? From time to time I am still asked if I can recommend a book on the Mass for the intelligent and interested Catholic. I hope that this modest book will be a good answer to that question. Many fine theologians and liturgical scholars have written excellent books on the Mass. Many of them, like Ralph Keifer in *To Give Thanks and Praise*, aim more to inform priests and/or liturgical musicians. I hope to provide a commentary that will serve, as it were, the other side of the altar. The appearance of *The Catechism of the*

Catholic Church and, more recently, a new edition of the *General Instruction on the Roman Missal* (2002) makes a book like this both practical and desirable.

The purpose of this book is threefold: to provide

1. A commentary on the Mass in light of the most recent official documents
2. A brief, up-to-date survey of the historical development of the Mass from the New Testament to the present
3. A reflection on the meaning of the Eucharist for us today

A word of caution: a work of this size and scope cannot pretend to treat each and every issue exhaustively, nor can it pretend to be the last word in theology. Actually, no book—whatever its size and scope—can pretend to be the last word in theology. By its very nature theology is the study of Christian faith and practice in particular times and places. The word *inculturation* is very popular today. Although the word is relatively new, the practice is as old as Christianity itself. Religious faith (and theology, which reflects on it) does not descend from heaven in a pure form that is merely translated into different languages and cultures. No. It is shaped by its reception in those very diverse cultures. This shouldn't be too difficult to appreciate in a religion that is so intimately bound up with embodiment—the very embodiment of God in our humanity. As we shall see, the celebration of the Mass and the sacrament of the Eucharist have everything to do with embodiment. Correctly understood, there is no other religion that gives such importance to the body, to our material world. The Christian task isn't to escape the world as though it were simply a vale of tears, as some approaches to spirituality seem to suggest. The task of the Christian is to cooperate with God in bringing the world back to God—to participate in the process of the Word of God taking flesh, living, dying and rising for the world's sake.

Christian theology and practice must always be embodied in particular cultures and specific times. Such adaptation requires careful discernment. For example, I have great reverence and respect for St. Thomas Aquinas. With St. Augustine he is certainly the greatest of all Christian theologians. But what made St. Thomas so great was not that he "figured Christianity out" once and for all, but that he applied the best knowledge and understanding of his own time to an astounding knowledge and appreciation of the Christian tradition. We honor someone like St. Thomas today, not by repeating everything he said (although much of it is still extremely valid and valuable) but by doing what he did: applying our best contemporary understanding to a thorough knowledge of the Christian tradition. And so we can begin to understand that tradition and traditionalism are not the same thing. (I often have qualms when people call themselves "traditionalists," meaning "defenders of the tradition." To defend the tradition is not to be old-fashioned but to appreciate the tradition in all of its richness and variety.)

For the very same reason that we cannot have a perennial theology—one that never changes—we also cannot possess a perennial liturgy. The history of the liturgy is a story of change and adaptation. Over the past forty years the Catholic Church has experienced a fairly radical change in its liturgical practice, largely because the previous five hundred years had been relatively changeless. This period has not been without difficulties, but I am confident that as we grow in our appreciation of the riches and the beauty of the liturgy, not to mention the vision of renewal flowing in the Second Vatican Council, we shall see an end to the "liturgy wars" and get down to the business of worshiping God and putting that worship into practice by our love of neighbor.

It is often said that the Mass is at the center of the Christian life. It's all the more important to take this notion seriously because it is the testimony of saints—people whose lives testify to the presence of God and the Christian message. In order to understand the centrality of the Mass more deeply, so that it doesn't become just another aphorism that we mouth politely and blithely, it is necessary to know something of its history, its origin in the ministry and person of Jesus and its liturgical elements and structure. Why, for example, do we have several readings from Scripture at every Mass? Why do we always read a passage from the Gospels last? Why is the eucharistic prayer called the center and highpoint of the celebration of the Eucharist? What difference does it make if communion is distributed from the tabernacle or consecrated at the Mass at which people are receiving? Why do we have more than one eucharistic prayer? Is it important that people are offered communion in both kinds—the Body and the Blood of Christ? Why did the Mass get its popular name from the dismissal *(missa)*? Why was it important to recover the exchange of peace? I hope that these questions will receive satisfactory answers in what follows.

The Mass is an objective act of worship by the Church. It has meaning and value in and of itself, but it is also a subjective act of worship of a particular community and the individuals who make up the community. Like any act of worship—or any other worthwhile human activity, like eating, working or lovemaking—some experiences of the Mass will be more significant than others. Perhaps some personal examples might help. On the evening of November 16, 1989, I was the scheduled presider for our community Mass at the Jesuit School of Theology at Berkeley (where I was teaching at the time). Earlier that day we received the awful news that six Jesuits, their housekeeper and her daughter had been murdered, most likely by army troops, in San Salvador at the

University of Central America. That evening our chapel over-
flowed with three or four times the usual number of people,
many of them from the other schools in the Graduate
Theological Union, our consortium. The air was electric, and
people hung on every word of the homily that I had (in the
meantime) asked a friend of the Salvadoran Jesuits, Fr. Marcello
Azevedo, S.J., to give. Or consider the evening of September
11, 2001. The monastery church near Weston Jesuit School
of Theology in Cambridge, Massachusetts (where I now
teach), was also filled—this time because of that morning's
shocking terrorist attacks on New York and Washington. The
monks had quickly and wisely changed the music for that
evening's eucharistic celebration. The vestments were purple
instead of green, and the prayers were appropriate to a time
of loss and suffering. There was no homily—only a reverential period of silence followed by ardent intercessions. The
Sunday that followed saw packed churches everywhere. These
experiences of the liturgy were especially poignant because
we had a heightened awareness of what was at stake.
Somehow on the occasions I have mentioned, as well as
sometimes at baptisms, weddings, funerals, ordinations or
other special occasions, Christ's free self-offering for the life
of the world that is celebrated at every Mass comes home to
us with particular clarity. I am probably romanticizing a bit,
but at times I think that the Christians of the early centuries
had an advantage on us since they celebrated their faith for
the most part as members of minority groups in their culture
and in times of sporadic persecution. I once had a student
who complained that in the early church it wasn't clear that
the people had much to do in the liturgy. It's true that our
scant reports don't tell us much about what we would call
active participation. (Historical sources often don't have good
answers to our questions.) At the same time, it seems to me

that it is hard to get more participative than putting your life on the line for what you believe.

It is unrealistic to expect that every Mass will have the same emotional impact for us as those special occasions. Sometimes people seem to expect each liturgy to be a "peak experience," but I don't think we can expect that. Often we need simply to be faithful in our celebration of the Lord's command to "do this in memory of me." Every now and then a routine Sunday liturgy can take us by surprise and lift us out of the doldrums of faith. When I served as a visiting priest at St. Paschal Baylon Church in Oakland, California, for a number of years, I was often taken aback when an ordinary Sunday Eucharist seemed to explode with faith and joy. Of course such things do not happen by accident. This particular community was nurtured and educated by an excellent and talented pastor. They were also well served by very competent liturgical musicians. Of course all the hard work and preparation in the world cannot make up for the power of the presence of God's Spirit and the faith that members of the assembly have received with joy.

We cannot expect every liturgy to knock us off our feet. At the same time I think we can expect liturgical celebrations filled with faith and reverence, and we can approach them confident in God's invitation, Christ's presence and the Spirit's power in our midst. We do not need every liturgy to be an earthshaking experience, but we do need to be able to find in every liturgy the source of our faith and hope and love. This is not always a matter of the emotion of the moment. For example, we don't feel joyful at funerals. Most people feel a mixture of loss, grief, sadness, sometimes even regret and guilt. At the same time we usually celebrate the Eucharist (Thanksgiving) at funerals— not because of our surface feelings but because of our more profound faith in the gift of life that God has given us and that we are confident God shares with our loved ones.

In addition, the liturgy is filled with a large number of (sometimes fairly obscure) elements. Although the minor details of the liturgy, like liturgical colors or vesture or the shape and size of the liturgical vessels, are not of great importance, at the same time the liturgy is made up of any number of details that we need to pay attention to. And so there is a kind of middle ground between carelessness about the liturgy (which is most often expressed by unpreparedness or sloppiness) and a neurotic consumption with details or the kind of smirking comment one can hear from people "in the know" who have caught some mistake. Many styles and approaches to liturgy (and especially to liturgical music and what I call the "choreography" of the liturgy) are valid and desirable. There are some boundaries, of course. We call them rubrics. Like canon law, rubrics are supposed to be the result of the corporate wisdom of God's people who need to protect their identity and activity in certain ways—as they have learned from experience. They are not supposed to be the imposition of arbitrary rules. (I like to tell the students to whom I teach presiding that rubrics are meant to protect the people of God from their idiosyncrasies. One of my primary rules for presiders is "Thou shalt not distract the people of God.") Just as there is an important distinction between tradition and traditionalism, so we must make a distinction between rubrics and rubricism. (The latter is an activity which indicates that its practitioner needs to find something more interesting to do.) Just as we need tradition, not traditionalism, so also we need rubrics but not rubricism.

My hope for you, the readers of this modest commentary, is that you will gain a deeper knowledge and appreciation for the celebration of the Mass and a greater conviction of its importance for our ordinary living-out of Christian faith in daily life. If that happens, then this work will have more than repaid the effort.

Food, Glorious Food

Ever since Eve ate apples, much depends on dinner.

—LORD BYRON

Byron's quip about food makes a fit beginning for considering the meaning of the Mass. After all, eating is the most fundamental of activities. Without food there is no life. And without sharing food, life does not seem to hold much significance. The poet Byron had good insight into the fact that eating and drinking are an important avenue into thinking about human history and the human condition.

One of the most pressing questions that people ask with regard to the Eucharist is, Why bother? Why should we come together week after week? If we believe in God (and particularly in Jesus Christ), why can't we practice our faith at home or communing with nature or by doing some worthwhile service for our neighbor instead of going to church? Surely praying at home and doing good works are able to provide some richer religious feelings than a (relatively) predictable liturgy. Even if we can be persuaded that going to church is a good idea, why does our service have to take the form of the same ritual of the Mass when perhaps some other religious service more directly relevant to our concerns might be arranged? Isn't the model of the twelve-step group with its sharing and spirituality a better recipe for twenty-first-century Christians? This book is intended both to respond to those questions and to deepen understanding of how the Christian liturgy of the Mass unfolds.

An easy answer to the questions, Why Church on Sunday? and Why the Mass? would simply be, Because Jesus told us to do it. At the Last Supper he said to his disciples, "Do this in memory of me"—and so Christians have been doing "this" one way or another ever since—especially in a communal way of Sunday, the day of resurrection. This response—that we are obeying Jesus' command—is certainly not incorrect, but it is inadequate, since it doesn't show how the Eucharist responds to some of the most fundamental issues and problems facing human beings both as individuals and as communities. The Liturgy Constitution has this to say about the Mass in particular:

> From the liturgy, therefore, particularly the eucharist, grace is poured forth upon us as from a fountain; the liturgy is the source for achieving in the most effective way possible human sanctification and God's glorification, the end to which all the Church's other activities are directed.[1]

Often referred to as "source and summit" language, this affirmation about the centrality of the Mass is a stunning statement about its role in Christian living. The point of this introductory chapter is to spell out the implications of this way of talking about the Eucharist as well as to show that the Mass goes right to the heart of the human predicament and is so central to Christian identity and mission that it is hard to imagine a church that calls itself "Catholic" without Sunday Eucharist. For Catholics the Eucharist is not simply *a* way of worshiping God, it is *the* privileged means of experiencing the presence of Jesus Christ and participating in his work of redeeming the world.

We have been reflecting on the Mass as a participation in the presence of Christ and his redeeming activity and as the source and summit of the Christian life. This language is a bit too religious to make sense without further explanation. It's all well and good to say that Jesus Christ has saved the world, but no matter how good the answer, we need to ask the question, Saved from what? Is there something about our human condition that really needs saving? The Christian answer to that question is yes. Human beings (as a whole and as individuals) are trapped in a sinful condition and unable to be united to God, the true source of life, by their own efforts.

I don't think we can get a handle on the significance of being saved in Jesus Christ without starting at the most fundamental level—our bodies. Because we are more than our bodies, human beings have always had a difficult time dealing with the limits that our bodies impose: we need food, drink, rest, we get sick, we grow old and inevitably we die. Our consciousness and our instincts tell us that we are more than this—but there's the rub—it's the givenness of our bodies that we cannot escape as we strive to be more. The French philosopher Pascal once said, "Anyone who wants to play the angel, ends up by playing the beast." In other words, we cannot escape our physicality. You might say—*outside the body there is*

BOX 1.1. WHAT'S IN A NAME?

Notice that the terms *Mass* and *Eucharist* are used interchangeably. The Eucharist has gone by many names throughout its history. Today *Eucharist* is most commonly used. It derives from the Greek noun *eucharistia,* which means "thanksgiving." Although the noun itself is not found in the New Testament, the verb *eucharistein* (to give thanks) is found, for example, in the Last Supper accounts (Matthew 26:27; Mark 14:23; Luke 22:17, 19; 1 Corinthians 11:24) and in the stories about the feeding of the multitudes (John 6:11). As we shall see in chapter 10, giving thanks is a governing motif of our celebration. The term *Mass* is derived from the Latin word *missa* for dismissal, as in the Latin dismissal formula: *Ite, missa est.* In chapter 9 we shall see how significant it is that one of the most popular and enduring names for our celebration is related to what we do when we leave it. Other names given to the Eucharist throughout history have related to various aspects of the celebration. Latin, Greek and Syriac have used terms for "offering" to accentuate the fact that the Eucharist is a sacrifice. At times, and especially by Protestants, the celebration has been called the "Lord's Supper" from the phrase used by St. Paul in 1 Corinthians 11:20. It has also been called "Holy Communion" to emphasize the goal that makes sense of this sacred meal. Finally, in the Gospel of Luke and the Acts of the Apostles it is referred to as "the breaking of the bread" (Luke 24:35; Acts 2:46).

no salvation. As embodied human beings neither can we escape the necessity of eating and drinking. At the same time, being more than our bodies means that we also strive for meaning and significance. The trap in the human condition is that we never consider enough to be enough—there has to be more. This instinct, strangely, leads to both economics and sacrifice, as the anthropologist Ernest Becker once observed.[2]

It is no accident that the story of the origin of sin in the Genesis account of creation centers around eating. It is possible to live without engaging in sexual relations, but it is not possible to live without eating and (for humans) without meaning. Margaret Visser has interpreted the use of table manners as a way of coming to terms with the violent impulses that need to be controlled when human beings sit down to eat together.[3] Notice how the Eden story combines eating and significance. The serpent says, "You will not die; for God knows that when you eat of it your eyes will be opened and you will be like God, knowing good and evil" (Genesis 3:4, NRSV). The first parents clearly have enough in the Garden of Eden, but they want more. And they don't want the "more" God's way; they want it their way. They do it by eating what is not theirs to eat—the fruit of the tree of knowledge of good and evil.

As psychologist Norman O. Brown put it, if eating is the form of the Fall it is also the form of Redemption.[4] And so the Eucharist represents the powerful antidote to the origin of sin. When the early-second-century bishop Ignatius of Antioch called the Eucharist "the medicine of immortality,"[5] he wasn't talking about some kind of magic potion but rather affirming the fact that partaking of the Eucharist is the antidote to the food taken in Eden.

What is sin, then, but a radical turning away from God and a turning in toward oneself in a desperate effort to achieve

self-significance? Sooner or later every sin comes down to this.
You could call it selfishness but I think it's better to call it self-
centeredness. The origin of this self-centeredness is a human
inability to let God be God. The original parents of the
Genesis story cannot trust God's word and they end up wal-
lowing in recrimination: "It's somebody else's fault." Some
early Christian writers considered this sinful condition not so
much one of deliberate disobedience of God as a sign of the
immaturity that Christ came to undo.

What happened because humankind *grasped* at being like
God is undone by Christ, who did just the opposite. In his
letter to the Philippians St. Paul quotes a very early Christian
hymn that contrasts the first and the second Adam:

> Let the same mind be in you that was in Christ Jesus
> who, though he was in the form of God,
> did not regard equality with God
> as something to be exploited (grasped),
> but emptied himself,
> taking the form of a slave,
> being born in human likeness.
> And being found in human form,
> he humbled himself
> and became obedient to the point
> of death—
> even death on a cross.
> Therefore God also highly
> exalted him. . . . (Philippians 2:5–9)

If sin is grasping, then redemption is letting go. If sin
means symbolically grabbing at food, then redemption means
sharing it and giving it away. Jesus accepted his creaturehood
with open hands as a gift. Ironically, being divine for Jesus

meant accepting humanity to the fullest. As has often been said, in revealing his divinity Jesus also reveals to us our humanity—our ultimate destiny. We shall see how this plays out further in chapter 10, when we reflect on the meaning of the Mass in light of its components. But now suffice it to say that the reality that the Mass manifests is the process of divine self-emptying in a ritual nutshell. There is a traditional Latin phrase that was used to praise the Incarnation of the Word of God: *O admirabile commercium!* It means "O marvelous exchange," referring to the fact that God took on human nature so that human beings could be united to God. The same exchange takes place in the Eucharist, as the resources of the earth receive God's word so that we receiving them (him) can be united to God. Jesus makes himself literally the food of Christians. And so what is potentially the source of sin and self-centeredness becomes the source of reversing sin. Yes, indeed, much does depend on dinner!

We can say that Jesus does what human beings on their own could not do: he accepts his existence as a gift from God and does the only thing one can do appropriately on receipt of a gift—say "thank you" both in word and deed. That acceptance of our human nature, that self-emptying, is precisely what we call Incarnation—the assumption of flesh and blood, real humanity with the exception of the self-centeredness/sinfulness of the human condition. It is extremely difficult for us today to appreciate that Christ is both fully divine and fully human (as we affirm every Sunday and major feast day in the Nicene Creed). Holding those two realities in balance has always been difficult for Christians, who seem to want to turn Jesus into either a God who merely appears to have a human body or an extraordinarily holy person and powerful teacher who leads us to God. I suspect that these concepts can't be resolved by intellectual categories but need to be played out in story—*the story* of the Gospel, which is played out Sunday after Sunday in the Liturgy of the Word and the Liturgy of the Eucharist.

This is why Eucharist, or "Thanksgiving," is such an apt name for what we do when we gather as Christians. The sharing of food and drink (the Body and Blood of the Lord) signifies the sharing of oneself, just as Jesus gave himself at the Last Supper in anticipation of his ultimate self-giving on the cross. The important thing to remember is that in giving his body and blood Jesus is not giving some*thing* but rather himself. At root what Jesus is saying is: "This is who I am for you—and who you must be for one another." The only appropriate way to respond is by our own self-giving. The Eucharist recapitulates the Christian life—but in a ritual way. This will become clearer in chapter 8 on the eucharistic prayer and in chapter 10 when we reflect further on the presence and the action (or sacrifice) of Christ that is celebrated in the Eucharist.

For now it is important to understand how the Eucharist responds to the human condition. By the repetitive pattern of entering into Christ's own self-giving, the Christian community participates in what we call the Paschal Mystery. The Christian word *Pascha* (Greek) is derived from the Hebrew word *Pesach* (or Passover) and refers to the Christian Passover as the event of the Lord's death and resurrection. The Paschal Mystery is the saving event of the world because it undoes the history of sin as grasping at being God. The beauty of the Eucharist is that it makes this event real by the very same activity that symbolized the difficulty in the first place—eating: the form of the Fall is the form of the Redemption. A traditional way of referring to the celebration of the Paschal Mystery is to speak of it as the eucharistic sacrifice. We shall come back to this idea, which is fundamental for understanding the Eucharist, but for now we need to acknowledge the difficulty

of the idea of sacrifice. It has been used so often to impose sac-
rifices on others that it often seems to have lost its value. But
I am speaking here of free self-sacrifice. The sacrifice that Christ
made once and for all on the cross and which is celebrated in
the Mass arose from his freedom. The same needs to be true
of us. As St. Paul put it beautifully: "I appeal to you, therefore,
brothers and sisters, by the mercies of God, to present your
bodies as a living sacrifice, holy and acceptable to God, which
is your true spiritual worship" (Romans 12:1).

Sacrifice is no longer the offering of animals or food and
drink, but the offering of oneself. Some anthropologists think
that sacrifice started out as human sacrifice. Understood in
this way, God's preventing Abraham from sacrificing Isaac in
Genesis 22 is actually a story about how animals (and subse-
quently other foodstuffs) were substituted for human sacrifice. But ultimately the death of Jesus shows us that true
sacrifice is not really about *killing* anybody or anything so
much as it is about offering oneself freely to God and to others in faith, hope and trust. In the end, that is what Christian
liturgy is all about.

At this point I hope you can see why the shared ritual
meal is such a fitting sacramental activity for Christians. The
shared meal is an antidote to the selfishness and violence that
could be signified by eating only for oneself. The shared
meal symbolizes the fact that acceptance and sharing constitute true humanity, and it reveals the fact that communal sharing in the context of faith in God is the true source of joy.
And since we share the fruits of creation in the consecrated
bread and wine, we also affirm the basic goodness of the
material creation so essential to the Catholic view of reality.
We Catholics have a wonderful sacramental realism because
we affirm the Incarnation so seriously—God's self-commitment
to the material world.

The rest of this book unfolds the insights that are presented in this chapter in a very condensed form. Chapter 2
summarizes the Eucharist in the New Testament. Chapter 3
gives a brief history of the Mass. The following chapters contain a commentary on the Mass. Chapters 4, 5 and 6 deal with
the entrance rite, the Liturgy of the Word and the lectionary
for Mass. Chapter 7 treats the rites that surround the preparation of the gifts. Chapter 8 is about the eucharistic prayer at
the center of the liturgy along with the presentation of the gifts
and the breaking of the consecrated bread and pouring of the
consecrated wine. Chapter 9 deals with the culmination of the
Mass—receiving Communion as an act of union with the Lord
and with one another at the same time. Chapter 10 consists of
a theological reflection based on our "reading" of the Mass
liturgy. Among other issues it deals with eucharistic sacrifice,
real presence (transubstantiation) and Mass intentions.

To sum up: celebrating the Mass is central to our identity
and mission as Christians because it means participating in a
ritual way in the self-offering of Christ for the life of the world.
Jesus Christ undertook this self-offering as the means to undo
"the sin of Adam and Eve," the origin and basis of sin in grasping at being God, often called the sin of pride. The opposite
of sin can be found in the community of the Church—the
gathering of those who know that Christ has become the center of their life and celebrate his message, his presence and his
activity as the Spirit empowers them to do sacramentally on a
regular basis. Christians don't participate in this saving activity of the Incarnate Christ by running away from the world
but, on the contrary, by letting Christ encounter them in their
most fundamental and intimately human activities.

Why bother with the Mass? I hope you have begun to get
the picture that we bother with the Mass because we "bother

with Jesus." The next two chapters unfold how Christians have celebrated Christ in the sacrament of the Eucharist from the New Testament right down to the present. Chapter 2 spells out the elements of that celebration as we experience it today.

Questions for Reflection

1. What moves me or leaves me cold in the celebration of the Mass? Why?
2. What's the connection between eating and drinking and the celebration of the Eucharist?
3. How does Jesus undo the sinfulness of the human condition?
4. How does the Mass relate to Jesus' person and activity?

The Eucharist in the New Testament

At the Last Supper, on the night when He was betrayed, our Savior instituted the eucharistic sacrifice of His Body and Blood. He did this in order to perpetuate the sacrifice of the Cross throughout the centuries until He should come again, and so to entrust to His beloved spouse, the Church, a memorial of His death and resurrection: a sacrament of love, a sign of unity, a bond of charity, a paschal banquet in which Christ is eaten, the mind is filled with grace, and a pledge of future glory is given to us.

—CONSTITUTION ON THE SACRED LITURGY, 47

Vatican II's *Constitution on the Sacred Liturgy* clearly points to the Last Supper as the institution of the Eucharist. As with most aspects of the New Testament, the origins of the Eucharist are much more complex. What kind of information can the New Testament give us about the Eucharist? Why is it important? What exactly do the various New Testament writings tell us about how to celebrate the Eucharist and what it means to do so? These are the questions that this chapter addresses.

Finding the Eucharist in the New Testament

First, I want to say something about what the New Testament can and cannot tell us. The various writings of the New Testament do not give us detailed rules or even information about the celebration of the Eucharist. For example, St. Paul deals with the Eucharist in two chapters (10–11) of his first letter to the Corinthians. The context (or genre) of the information provided there is that of a letter dealing with community problems. Paul presumes that the Corinthians know how to celebrate the Eucharist and uses various aspects of the celebration to make a point—first about food offered to idols and second about divisions within the community. Today we know that the Gospels are not straightforward narrative accounts or biographies in the modern sense but rather theological proclamations of the good news from and in the person of Jesus of Nazareth. If everything the New Testament says about the celebration of the Eucharist were clear, we would not have had twenty centuries of debate and discussion about its meaning. Thus in the context of other concerns the New Testament writers give hints as to the meaning of the Eucharist. Each reference to the Eucharist is also affected by the practice of the community in which and for which a particular piece was written.

In other words, the liturgy has affected the story. In this way we can understand why the four narratives of the Last Supper differ. They reflect slightly different liturgical practices.

The New Testament does not provide a detailed outline of liturgical practices nor does it give us a definitive handbook of doctrine and morals. It is the faithful and inspired witness of the Church to God's revelation in Jesus of Nazareth. This is why Christianity is not a "religion of the book" in the same way that Islam is. Revelation is primarily found in the person of Jesus. The Bible is the Church's book—and as such it bears witness to that revelation. Catholics have always insisted that the Bible needs to be interpreted by living authority in the power of the Holy Spirit. Therefore a literalistic or fundamentalistic reading of the biblical texts is erroneous. We shall see how the liturgy itself acts as a corrective to fundamentalism when we consider the Liturgy of the Word.

In addition, the New Testament texts must always be read in light of the Old Testament. Christian faith is the legitimate heir of the faith of Israel. In this sense, Christianity and Judaism are siblings rather than parent and child. Since rabbinic Judaism (the form of Judaism that we are familiar with today) does not really begin until after the fall of the Jerusalem temple in 70 A.D., Christianity could be considered the older religious faith. Both claim the faith of Israel. The Jews are not our ancestors in the faith as much as brothers and sisters who interpret the same tradition in vastly different ways. And so we need to reaffirm the Jewishness of Jesus when we try to understand his religious practice. (I will, however, follow the usual convention and speak of Jesus' contemporaries as "Jews.")

The New Testament Texts

As I suggest above, there are allusions to the Eucharist in several places in the New Testament, the most prominent of which are the narratives of institution. There are four places where these are inserted: in each of the three Synoptic Gospels (Matthew, Mark and Luke—called synoptic because they follow the same basic structure and content) and in St. Paul's first letter to the Corinthians. John's Gospel has no institution narrative but a long discourse on the "Bread of Life" in chapter 6. Let us begin with the institution narratives, which are laid out in table 2.1.

Even the most cursory glance at table 2.1 reveals differences among these four narratives. The columns are arranged to show that Matthew and Mark have similarities and that 1 Corinthians 11 and Luke also have a family resemblance. Scholars have taken to calling the Matthew/Mark tradition "Palestinian" and the Paul/Luke tradition "Antiochene," from the city that Paul took as his missionary launching pad. None of these narratives is exactly what we hear in the Church's eucharistic prayers either. As a matter of fact (with the possible exception of an Ethiopian prayer that I have not been able to track down), no traditional eucharistic prayer has ever reproduced one of the New Testament institution narratives verbatim. The traditional institution narrative of the Roman Canon, however, was edited in the Vatican II reform to correspond somewhat more closely to the Scriptures.

Eating and Drinking in the Ancient World

Before we go into the similarities and differences in these narratives, we must deal with food and meals in the ancient world. In ancient, indeed in all traditional, societies, food and whom you share it with are extremely important. In other words, Who eats what with whom? was an extremely important question in the ancient world. In the first place, ritual purity was affected by the persons you ate with. Jews could contract ritual impurity (i.e., the inability to offer sacrifice) by

TABLE 2.1. ACCOUNTS OF THE LAST SUPPER

Palestinian Tradition	Antiochene Tradition		
Matthew 26:26–29	Mark 14:22–25	Luke 22:15–20	1 Corinthians 11:23–26
While they were eating, Jesus took a loaf of bread, and after blessing it he broke it, gave it to the disciples and said, 'Take, eat; this is my body.' Then he took a cup, and after giving thanks he gave it to them, saying, 'Drink from it all of you; for this is my blood of the covenant; which is poured out for many for the forgiveness of sins. I tell you I will never again drink of this fruit	While they were eating, he took a loaf of bread, and after blessing it he broke it, gave it to them, and said, 'Take; this is my body.' Then he took a cup, and after giving thanks he gave it to them, and all of them drank from it. He said to them, 'This is my blood of the covenant, which is poured out for many. Truly I tell you, I will never drink again of the fruit of the vine until	He said to them, 'I have eagerly desired to eat this Passover with you before I suffer; for I tell you I will not eat it until it is fulfilled in the kingdom of God.' Then he took a cup, and after giving thanks he said: 'Take this, and divide it among yourselves; for I tell you that from now on I will not drink of the fruit of the vine until the kingdom of God comes.'	For I received from the Lord what I also handed on to you, that the Lord Jesus on the night when he was betrayed took a loaf of bread, and when he had given thanks, he broke it and said, 'This is my body that is for you. Do this in remembrance of me.' In the same way he took the cup also, after supper, saying, 'This cup is the new covenant in my blood. Do this, as often as you drink it, in remembrance of me.'

Palestinian Tradition		Antiochene Tradition	
Matthew 26:26–29	Mark 14:22–25	Luke 22:15–20	1 Corinthians 11:23–26
of the vine until that day when I drink it new with you in my Father's kingdom.'	that day when I drink it new in the kingdom of God.'	Then he took a loaf of bread, and when he had given thanks, he broke it and gave it to them, saying, 'This is my body [which is given for you. Do this in remembrance of me.' And he did the same with the cup after supper saying, 'This cup that is poured out for you is the new covenant in my blood.'] *The bracketed section is missing in many manuscripts*	

any number of means. It was probably easier to contract such impurity than to catch a cold when a bug is going around in the winter. One way was to touch something impure, like a corpse, another to be under the same roof as an impure person. A third way was to share a meal with someone in the state of impurity. Some writers have suggested that Jesus spent a great deal of his time in a state of ritual impurity. In fact he seems to have been quite concerned with redrawing the lines of what impurity meant (see Mark 7:1–30).

Second, food was scarce in the ancient world. In particular meat was scarce and usually shared only when a sacrifice had been made. In regard to the eucharistic banquet we need to remember that Jesus' teaching and actions took place in a world of poverty where a banquet would be truly extravagant because people were hungry most of the time. Moreover, traditional societies did not know the neat separation that we make between religious and social aspects of life. Feasts of any kind would inevitably have a religious character.

Third, Jewish meals were framed by formal blessings. There are two ways of speaking about blessings. The first is to recognize how God blesses people and things, as in the well-known priestly blessing of Numbers 6:24–26 ("The Lord bless you and keep you; the Lord make his face to shine upon you . . ."). A second way reverses the direction. In other words, God is blessed for something or someone. To "bless God" means to acknowledge or praise God for what God has done. We adapt this Jewish notion of blessing in our formulas at the presentation of the gifts and preparation of the altar at Mass: "Blessed are *you*, Lord God of all creation. . . ." To understand this meaning of blessing is crucial for understanding the Eucharist. The pious Jew of Jesus' time blessed God continually, just like the charismatic Christian of today, who tends to say "Thank you, Jesus" in every conceivable situation. God is blessed morning, noon and night. What is more, nothing seems to be accessible to men and women unless God is blessed for it. There is a profound spirituality here and it lies at the basis of the Mass: things are good and holy for us only when we put them in the proper perspective—when we recognize God as their source. You can see how well this relates to the "human dilemma" outlined in chapter 1. It is only when we recognize the gift character of creation that we can overcome the trapped nature of the human condition. And Christians give a personal name to that recognition: Jesus Christ.

Every formal Jewish meal was framed by blessings, especially a blessing for the first cup of wine at the beginning, for the bread broken and shared and finally for a second cup at the end of the meal. This last was called "the cup of blessing," and the major blessing prayer seems to have been associated with the end of the meal. The Jewish word for blessing is *berakah*. It comes from the root of the verb BRK, meaning "to bless" and is found as *berakoth* in the plural and as *birkat-ha-mazon* when it means the grace after meals. One cannot understand our eucharistic prayers without recognizing that they have their origins in Jewish formulas of blessing and prayers of thanksgiving *(todah)* for favors that God has granted. Thus in the accounts of the Last Supper when we read that Jesus "said the blessing" or "gave thanks," we realize he was doing what any pious Jew would have done. I might note here some disagreement with the popular New Revised Standard Version (hereafter NRSV) translation of Matthew 26:26 and Mark 14:22. Both presume that Jesus blessed the bread, whereas the participle *eulogēsas* is better translated "saying the blessing."

The Last Supper: A Passover?

It is often asserted that the Last Supper was a particular kind of meal: a Passover meal. Passover was one of three great annual feasts for the Jews. On these feasts adult males were expected to make a pilgrimage to Jerusalem. Passover took place on the evening of the first full moon of the first (spring) month of the year (14 Nisan). Its origins lie in a sacrifice of lambs for protection of the flock as well as the first wheat harvest of spring (Feast of Unleavened Bread). In the Bible it becomes the feast that celebrates the liberation of the Jews from bondage in Egypt.

There is no doubt that Jesus died at the time of Passover, but there is a discrepancy in the Gospel accounts. For Matthew, Mark and Luke (the Synoptics) the Last Supper takes place on the evening after the Passover lambs are slaughtered and is therefore a true Passover meal. In John's Gospel, on the other hand, Jesus dies at the same time that the Passover lambs are being sacrificed and therefore the meal held on the night before could not have been a Passover. Scholars have debated this discrepancy for decades—without a solution in sight. The best that can be said with certainty is that the Last Supper took place in the atmosphere of Passover and that the disciples of Jesus came to understand that Jesus himself was the true Passover, as St. Paul puts it in 1 Corinthians 5:7, "For Christ, our paschal lamb, has been sacrificed."

The blessings *(berakoth)* that frame the Passover meal would have been used at any formal Jewish meal. (The exception is a special cup symbolizing the coming of Elijah the prophet of the end time. In any case mention of this cup does not figure in the Last Supper accounts.) Therefore the Passover Seder does not necessarily tell us anything about the roots of our Eucharist. As we shall see, the origins of the Eucharist we celebrate go beyond the Last Supper itself.

BOX 2.1. A CHRISTIAN SEDER?

In recent years it has become popular in some communities to celebrate a sort of Christian Passover Seder in an attempt to have Christians experience the Last Supper as Jesus himself would have celebrated. (Seder is the Hebrew word for "order" and so means the way the meal is conducted.) These celebrations are praiseworthy for a number of reasons:

- They move people to enter into the experience of Jesus and his disciples.
- They help us appreciate the affinities we have with our Jewish brothers and sisters.
- They clarify some of the origins of our eucharistic celebrations.

On the other hand such celebrations have some drawbacks:

- They tend to be celebrated on Holy Thursday, thus obscuring the fact that the real Christian celebration of Passover is the Easter (Paschal) Vigil, which culminates the great three days (Triduum).
- We do not really know the contours of the Passover celebration in the first century, since all of our Jewish sources come from the second century or later.

Therefore it would probably be better for Christians to accept invitations to Jewish homes for their own Passover Seders and to put their liturgical efforts into celebrating the Paschal Triduum as well as possible.

The Last Supper in Paul

St. Paul's first letter to the Corinthians is certainly the oldest literary witness to the institution narrative. (This begs the question of whether *oral* traditions behind the other narratives may be earlier.) The context for Paul's mention of the institution of the Eucharist by Christ is the factionalism and inequity in the communal meals of the Christians at Corinth. We shall come back to this at the end of the chapter. Paul situates the narrative on the night that Jesus was betrayed. There are a number of obvious differences between the account of Paul (and Luke as well) and Matthew/Mark:

- Paul has "this is the new covenant in my blood" rather than "this is my blood of the covenant.
- Paul has the command to repeat: "Do this in remembrance of me."
- The Pauline formula over the cup reads "for you" whereas Matthew/Mark have "for many" (which in Greek means "for all"—see chapter 8).
- Paul adds a phrase that relates the celebration of the Lord's Supper to proclaiming the death of the Lord.
- Paul mentions the fact that the meal intervened between the thanksgiving prayers over the bread and over the cup. He uses the verb "to give thanks" twice instead of the Matthew/Mark pattern of bless/give thanks.

Clearly the same story underlies all of these accounts, but they have been transmitted by different oral traditions and most probably affected by different liturgical practice. For example, Paul may need to remind his Greek audience that Jews separated the blessing of the bread and cup with the meal proper, though the circumstances seem to suggest that he wants to separate the celebration of the Eucharist from the unjust Corinthian meals at which some were fed and others left out. Each tradition seems to pick up a different scriptural reference to the relation between Jesus' blood and the covenant. The "new covenant in my blood" is a reference to Jeremiah 31:31, whereas the "blood of the covenant" most probably refers to Exodus 24:8, the blood that Moses sprinkled on the people in preparation for receiving the Law. One could add that whatever the specific biblical reference, the notion of covenant (the agreement that God makes with his people on his own initiative and that binds them to him) links the Last Supper to *the* Israelite feast of covenant renewal—Pentecost, or the Feast of Weeks, which was celebrated seven weeks after Passover. This feast originally celebrated the end of the spring wheat harvest and eventually came to celebrate the giving of the Law to Moses on Mount Sinai (Exodus 19–20).

The Gospel Narratives

Despite these differences we can conclude the following from the New Testament institution narratives:

- All of the authors understand Jesus to be giving himself (body and blood) to his disciples by identifying himself with the bread of the meal.
- The reference to blood clearly indicates that the authors understood that Jesus was relating this sacred meal to his suffering and death; it is a sacrificial motif. Participating in the cup is somehow participating in Jesus' fate, which the reader of the Gospel knows is not only passion and death but also resurrection and victory.
- Frequently people refer to the elements of the Eucharist as "ordinary" bread and wine, often out of a desire to

substitute ordinary food and drink of a particular
region as dynamic equivalents for wheat bread and
grape wine. But the dynamic equivalents for the elements of the Last Supper would not be ordinary food
and drink but rather ordinary food and festive drink.
Wine was not an everyday staple for the Israelites of
Jesus' time. The wine of the Last Supper also suggests
festive joy, another important aspect of the legacy that
Jesus is leaving behind.

- The narratives themselves do not necessarily give us
  any indication of how they were used in the liturgy.
- For the Synoptic Gospels the Last Supper acts as a kind
  of prelude to the entire Passion narrative. It is like an
  opera overture that states all of the main themes.

One of the most significant terms for the future of eucharistic theology is embedded in the Pauline/Lukan accounts of the
Last Supper. The word in Greek is *anamnesis*, and it has no easy
equivalent in English. It translates the Hebrew word *zikkaron*,
from the root ZKR, "to remember." The term means a good
deal more than the simple English phrase "do this in memory
of me" suggests. To us moderns memory is a very subjective
or psychological idea, but for the ancients it meant a good deal
more. The word "memorial" comes closer to the objectivity
connoted by both the Greek and Hebrew terms. An instruc-
tive parallel can be found in Deuteronomy 26:1–11, the offering of the first fruits of the grain harvest in the Feast of Weeks,
the covenant renewal feast mentioned above. After the priest
receives the offering the one making it says:

> A wandering Aramean was my ancestor; he went down
> into Egypt and lived there as an alien, few in number, and
> there he became a great nation, mighty and populous.

> When the Egyptians treated us harshly and afflicted us, by imposing hard labor on us, we cried to the Lord, the God of our ancestors; the Lord heard our voice and saw our affliction, our toil, and our oppression. The Lord brought us out of Egypt with a mighty hand and an outstretched arm, with a terrifying display of power, and with signs and wonders; and he brought us into this place and gave us this land, a land flowing with milk and honey. So now I bring the first of the fruit of the ground that you, O Lord, have given me.

Notice that the one making the sacrifice identifies himself with his ancestors. What happened to them, happened to us. This is the key to *anamnesis*. We are not speaking of a dead event but rather an event that we still live in. Second, *anamnesis* means doing something as a response to this memory—in this case making the offering of grain. Third, in Jesus' command to "do this as my memorial" the operative phrase is "as my memorial." As Gregory Dix pointed out, those at the Last Supper would have "done," that is, participated in, a meal that included the blessings in any case, but now they are to do it in a significantly new way—to make *anamnesis* of Jesus. In terms of the New Testament origins of the Eucharist it is very important to remember that very little changed in terms of the form of Jewish feasting but a great deal changed in terms of what (or better who) was celebrated.

The Meal Ministry of Jesus in Luke

Now let us turn to Luke's account of the Last Supper and his stories of Jesus at table. At least two aspects of Luke's account of the institution of the Eucharist call for comment. In the first place Luke seems to come closest to describing typical

Jewish meal practice by placing a blessing of the cup at the very beginning of the meal. And so, Luke frames the meal with Jesus' vow to refrain from feasting until the kingdom is inaugurated at the beginning, and what New Testament scholar Xavier Léon-Dufour calls the "testamentary tradition" at the end. That testamentary tradition is the second special aspect of Luke's treatment. After Jesus has blessed and passed the second cup to his disciples he predicts his betrayal. At this point Luke inserts material that comes much earlier in Matthew and Mark: a brief discourse on service and about what it means to be great. This, Léon-Dufour claims, brings the Eucharist into intimate relation with service of others. Chapter 13 in John's Gospel does something similar when Jesus leaves the foot washing as a testament to his disciples' need to serve one another. For Luke, therefore, one cannot separate liturgy from the Christian life.

In addition Luke's Gospel has a large number of dinner scenes. Jesus' table fellowship is clearly an important part of his ministry. Eugene Laverdiere counts ten meal scenes in Luke's Gospel. Seven of these precede the Last Supper, for example, at the homes of Levi (5:27–39), Martha (10:38–42) and Zacchaeus (19:1–10). These meal scenes show how Jesus exercises a ministry of reconciliation, how he redraws lines of belonging and how he celebrates the dawning even now of the reign of God.

Perhaps the most poignant of the meals in Luke's Gospel is the supper at Emmaus (24:13–35) on the evening of the resurrection. The story begins with Jesus meeting Cleopas and another disciple (a woman?) on the road as they are walking to Emmaus some seven miles from Jerusalem. Full of despair and failing to recognize him, these disciples tell Jesus how their hopes have been dashed. They do not even understand the message of the women who had been at the tomb—that he was alive. They expected a corpse and nothing, it seems, could change their expectation. Jesus opens up the (Old Testament) Scriptures to them with regard to his own identity and mission. They stop at an inn for the night and persuade him to stay with them. In the familiar gesture of the breaking of bread (and presumably the blessing that goes with it) they recognize him and he vanishes. Straightaway they return to Jerusalem and tell the other disciples "what had happened on the road, and how he had been made known to them in the breaking of the bread" (v. 35). This story makes three important points about celebrating the Eucharist among the early Christians—points that are still quite relevant for us today.

- It is necessary to have the Scriptures unfolded for us through the "lens" of Jesus and what he has accomplished.
- It is the action of breaking bread—brokenness and sharing—that reveals the identity of the Lord Jesus.
- Recognizing Jesus in the breaking of bread demands a response in action on the part of the disciples; they in turn must announce the good news.

The two disciples on the road to Emmaus thought that Jesus was a corpse. Their commonsense expectation was surprisingly reversed by the *sacramental* action of the breaking of bread. Christians know Jesus is alive in this sacramental activity.

The Miraculous Feedings

We have already seen that meals formed a large part of Jesus' ministry in the Gospel accounts. In a meal of a different sort Jesus feeds thousands of people who are stranded and hungry. There are two versions of this story in Mark's Gospel. The first takes place in chapter 6 where the location is Galilee, not far from Jesus' hometown of Nazareth. The setting for the second, chapter 8, is the non-Israelite territory of the Decapolis (ten cities), to the east of the Sea of Galilee. These locations are most likely the key to understanding why there are two versions of the same story. In the first miraculous feeding there are twelve baskets left over, and in the second there are seven. Twelve is the number of the tribes of Israel and seven a number that symbolized completeness in the ancient world. And so in the first story the number twelve signifies that the banquet of the end time has come to Israel. In the second salvation is being extended to the whole world— even non-Jews. Therefore, it seems that the Gospel writer meant to show that Jesus' kingdom meal was meant both for Israel and for the whole world.

How does this relate to the Eucharist? Each version of the story (Mark 6:34–44; 8:14–21; Matthew 14:13–21; Luke 9:10–17; John 6:1–13) employs the same verbs found in the Last Supper narratives—Jesus took, blessed, broke and gave. We shall see later how these became the backbone of the eucharistic celebration. The Gospel writers seem to understand the miraculous feedings to be a foretaste of the Eucharist. The stories certainly contain echoes of God's feeding of Israel in Isaiah 40:11, the manna in the wilderness (Exodus 16:13–35) and Elijah's feeding one hundred people with twenty loaves of barley (2 Kings 4:42–44). It might even be possible that Jesus himself made the connection between meals that signaled the coming of God's Reign (the banquet of the end time) and the Eucharist in which that Reign becomes identified with his very self. The Gospel of John tells us that Jesus distributes the bread directly to the people; in the Synoptics he gives it to the disciples to distribute. This may be an indication of Jesus' more direct relationship to the believer in the Fourth Gospel. John's account also leaves out the verb for "breaking" the bread. This could possibly signal that John's understanding of the Eucharist is more closely related to the idea of nourishment than to the Passion, death and resurrection of Jesus.

The Bread of Life in the Gospel of John

We have already noted that there is no account of the institution of the Eucharist in John's Gospel. On the other hand, chapter 6 contains a lengthy discourse on the "Bread of Life." The setting follows the miraculous feeding and the appearance of Jesus to his disciples on the storm-tossed Sea of Galilee. Chapter 6 has been much debated, with some scholars seeing an integral discourse and others seeing the hand of a later editor with sacramental interests interpolating eucharistic material into the end of the discourse. In any case, chapter 6 as we have it can be divided into three sections:

- Verses 25–34 set up the scene in typical Johannine fashion with mistaken questions leading to profound answers on the part of Jesus.
- Verses 35–51b are a kind of rabbinic commentary (midrash) on Psalm 78:24 ("He gave them bread from heaven to eat"). Here the bread from heaven seems to be Jesus himself as the personification of divine wisdom.
- Verses 51c–58 are clearly eucharistic with their references to eating (Gk. *trogein*, chewing) the flesh (Gk. *sarx*) of the Son of Man and drinking his blood.
- Verses 59–71 are not really part of the discourse but report that a number of disciples abandon Jesus because this teaching is too much for them. Peter

affirms: "Lord, to whom can we go? You have the
words of eternal life" (v. 68).

Note that the entire discourse lacks any reference to
wine. Perhaps it was taken for granted or perhaps the early
Johannine communities celebrated the Eucharist with water.
Over the centuries theologians have debated whether or not
the last section refers to the Eucharist at all. The problem
was raised with particular urgency by the Swiss reformer
Huldrych Zwingli (1484–1531), who insisted that Jesus'
words to the disciples in verse 63 ("It is the Spirit that gives
life; the flesh is useless") require a purely spiritual understanding of eucharistic presence. Martin Luther (1483–1546),
on the other hand, who had a very traditional understanding
of the presence of Christ in the Eucharist, concluded that
the discourse was about Jesus as the Word rather than the
Eucharist. Zwingli was the most radical of the Protestant
reformers. He emphasized the believer's spiritual relationship
to the Lord at the expense of the material and sacramental.
But it seems clear that the Gospel writer intended to refer
explicitly to the Eucharist at the end of the chapter. If this is
indeed the case, then we can see a subtle allusion in this chapter to the sequence: Word/Eucharist, which becomes a hall-
mark of Christian liturgy.

Paul, the Eucharist and Community

This survey of what the New Testament has to tell us about
the origins and the meaning of the Mass concludes with a
reflection on St. Paul's profound teaching about the Body of
Christ: Church *and* Eucharist. In 1 Corinthians 10 Paul introduces the subject of eucharistic communion into an argument
about eating meat that was sacrificed in pagan rituals. The

chapter begins with a warning about misusing the freedom that comes from believing in Jesus for the majority of the Israelites perished in the wilderness even though they were "baptized into Moses in the cloud and in the sea, and all ate the same spiritual food, and all drank the same spiritual drink" (1 Corinthians 10:2–3). In other words, being baptized and sharing in Holy Communion doesn't guarantee salvation. It all depends where your true communion lies. Therefore Paul introduces the notion that sharing the "cup of blessing" and partaking of the "bread which we break" constitute a real participation (Gk. *koinonia*) in the Body and Blood of Christ. Paul has a very profound sense of the Church as the Body of Christ—one which is in the process of being recovered today as we appreciate anew the ecclesial dimensions of the Eucharist.

In a similar way Paul continues in chapter 11 with some correctives to the communal life of the Corinthian Christians. He begins with advice of covering the head in the assembly. He moves on to a much weightier question: how the Corinthians conduct themselves at the Lord's Supper. Paul is, to say the least, extremely critical of Corinthian meal practice. When they assemble for the Lord's Supper it seems that some eat and drink without regard for those who come later and are left out. He therefore criticizes their practice and says "it is not really to eat the Lord's Supper" (11:20). In this context he introduces the account of the Last Supper that we dealt with earlier in this chapter. In other words, lack of equitable sharing (we could call it social justice) is directly contrary to participating in the Eucharist. Paul goes on to say: "For all who eat and drink without discerning the body; eat and drink judgement against themselves." Some commentators have interpreted "the body" here not so much as the eucharistic body of the Lord as the Church as the Body of Christ. In the Pauline context that interpretation makes a great deal of sense.

Paul is not trying to answer questions about the relation between bread and wine and the presence of Christ. Those particular questions arise many centuries later. He is, rather, writing about what it means to be a community (church) that assembles to celebrate with integrity who the Lord is and what the Lord has done.

Summary

What have we learned from the New Testament that can help us understand the meaning of the Mass and how we celebrate it?

1. The New Testament is too rich to be confined to a single pattern or theology of the Eucharist. Although we need to look for common patterns, it is important not to homogenize them too quickly.
2. The mere fact of eating/drinking and ordinary table sharing has profound religious implications. For this reason table sharing is an extremely important aspect of Israel's experience and of the practice and ministry of Jesus.
3. The earliest community celebrations of union in and with Christ are heavily determined by Jewish festive meal practice, including the prayer forms of blessing *(berakah)* and thanksgiving *(todah)*. In particular, the Eucharist in the New Testament has resonances with the celebration of Passover and Pentecost.
4. The Gospels of Matthew, Mark and Luke, as well as Paul's first letter to the Corinthians, associate the celebration of the Last Supper with Christ's redemptive death—especially by means of the cup of his blood, which relates to the idea of his sacrifice.

5. While the New Testament texts were not written to answer later theological questions about the presence of Christ in the bread and the wine or the manner of their transformation, they quite clearly point to a very realistic identification of the bread and wine with the Body and Blood of the Lord.

6. There are different theological accents in the various New Testament eucharistic texts. The Synoptics and St. Paul emphasize the connection between the Last Supper and Jesus' salvific death. John's Gospel concentrates on the intimate union between the believer and Jesus through the "Bread of Life." The Acts of the Apostles stress the joyful fellowship of the earliest communities in "the breaking of the bread" and their recognition thereby of the Risen Lord in their midst.

7. Each of these themes and accents brings a richness to our understanding of Christ's self-gift to the Church, which is the Eucharist.

Conclusion

On the night before he died, the Lord Jesus gave his disciples a way of truly experiencing his person and his mission. He gave them himself as the food and drink that are not grasped from the tree in the Garden of Eden, but rather freely given because of the tree of free self-giving, the Cross. Summing up his ministry of feeding and symbolizing God's lavish banquet at the end of time, he showed there is no way to salvation except through the free sharing of what we cannot possibly live without—food—and he identified himself with this sharing. "I am for you" he says in the Eucharist. And every time you participate in me you also share in my fate and commit yourself to being for others.

Let us see how this plays out in the development of the Christian Eucharist in history.

Questions for Reflection

1. What does the Jewish notion of *berakah* refer to? Why is it so important for understanding the Eucharist?
2. What do the differences between the four accounts of the Lord's Supper in the New Testament reveal?
3. Why does St. Mark's Gospel have two different reports of the feeding of the multitude?
4. What is distinctive about the way St. John's Gospel deals with the Eucharist?
5. In what context does St. Paul speak of the institution of the Lord's Supper?

A (Very) Brief History
of the Mass

The purpose of this brief history of the development of the Mass, a development that is extremely rich and complex, is to show how the basic pattern of Liturgy of the Word and Eucharist has taken diverse shapes in different cultures and historical periods. There is no one pristine or perfect form of the Mass, for the Church recognizes the value and importance of a number of different liturgical rites— Byzantine, Coptic, Armenian and so forth. Since my aim in this book is to promote a better understanding of the Eucharist that Roman Catholics celebrate today, I cannot treat the development of these other rites extensively, which is not to minimize their importance. First, I present an overview of the development of the Mass in four periods leading up to our contemporary celebration:

- The primitive Church
- From Constantine to the rise of Islam
- The medieval Mass
- After the Council of Trent

A great deal happened during each of these major blocks of time. It is somewhat fatuous to talk of the Middle Ages (some nine hundred years in this scheme) but, with caution, some generalizations can be made. Because so much happened in each period, I shall follow a basic outline for the sake of convenience:

- The physical and temporal setting
- Structure of the liturgy
- Praying and singing

The Primitive Church

We have already seen (in chapter 2) that the New Testament gives very little information as to precisely how the Eucharist was celebrated. We do know that its origins were tied up with Jewish forms of praying and there was likely some form of proclamation of the Word. Since chapter 14 of 1 Corinthians, with its description of prophecy, tongues and hymn singing, follows chapters 10–11 with their references to the Lord's Supper, it may be that, at least in some places, such a "Liturgy of the Word" followed the sacred meal just as in Hellenistic *symposia* of the Greek culture of the time. These *symposia* were festive occasions that included extended conversation after a

BOX 3.1. **RITES**

Different styles and forms of liturgical celebration grew up around the major cities or regions of the Roman Empire. These liturgies developed into the classic rites of Christian worship. Antioch in Syria and Jerusalem became the center of the West Syrian Rite. The Coptic Rite was centered in Alexandria, Egypt. Edessa became the home of the East Syrian Rite, which migrated to India to become the Malabar Rite. Armenia and Georgia also developed independent rites. The great east Roman capital, Constantinople (modern Istanbul), was home to the most influential of the Eastern rites: the Byzantine Rite, which became the major rite of Greece, Russia and much of Eastern Europe. The various rites were not hermetically insulated from one another. A good deal of borrowing and cross-fertilization took place.

In the West the most important city by far was Rome, from which spread the Roman Rite. By the eleventh century the Roman Rite covered Western and Southern Europe. Other rites, the Gallican (France) and Mozarabic or Visigothic (Spain), gradually disappeared or could be found only in isolated locales. Variants of the Roman Rite like the Ambrosian Rite in Milan and Northern Italy or the Sarum (Salisbury) Rite in England also survived.

At times rites are confused with churches. Different churches can use the same rite. For example, the Orthodox churches of Greece and Russia share the Byzantine Rite with Greek Catholics and Ruthenians.

meal. We have more evidence from the first three centuries but still no texts of the full liturgy.

Physical and Temporal Setting

The architectural setting of Christian worship in the first three centuries was somewhat modest. Most of the evidence suggests that private homes were used for the gathering of the Christian community. Sometimes, as at Dura-Europos in Syria on the eastern frontier of the Roman Empire, a wall was broken down to expand the community's gathering space. Christians did gather in the catacombs (cemeteries) for eucharistic celebrations, but not because they were hiding from the police. Pagans, Christians and Jews alike celebrated communal meals at the graves of their loved ones. The Christian community meal par excellence was the Eucharist. In particular the graves of the martyrs (who had died for their faith) were marked and became the sites of large shrines after Christianity became legal. In places where there were many Christians some public buildings (basilicas) came to be used for Christian worship even before the end of the persecutions. Some Roman emperors and local officials carried out sporadic persecutions of the Christians in the first three centuries of the Christian era. These persecutions took place because Christians were perceived as "atheists"—nonbelievers in the traditional religion that supported the empire and its leaders. The most severe persecutions took place under the Emperor Decius (c. 250) and Diocletian (c. 303).

How did the Lord's *Supper* come to be celebrated in the morning? The earliest Christian celebrations took place in the evening with the Christian blessing *(berakah)* over the bread and a blessing over the cup both before and after a meal. We find this pattern in a first (or early second) century catechetical document, *Didache* 9–10. *Didache* ("The Teaching of the Twelve Apostles") consisted of a handbook of moral instruction followed by some directions for worship and church leadership.

When the meal dropped from the celebration is not altogether clear. In some (non-Jewish Christian) communities like Corinth, the meal may have disappeared fairly quickly—especially given the inequalities that Paul complains of. We do know that an early-second-century Roman governor in Asia Minor, Pliny, reports about Christian gatherings in the morning. But even the often quoted information provided by Justin Martyr in his *First Apology* (c. 155) does not tell us at what time the Christians at Rome celebrated. Like the texts of the New Testament that we considered in chapter 2, the early Christian writers were not concerned to describe the details of the liturgy. Justin's description of the liturgy comes in the course of his explanation (apology) of the harmlessness of Christianity.

On the fast days (Wednesdays and Fridays) many early Christian communities broke their fast with the Eucharist. Eventually this practice became customary (and then mandatory) for all celebrations of the Eucharist. Fasting was a practice that was taken over from Judaism. The Jews fasted on Mondays and Thursdays. Self-discipline in the areas of eating and sexuality was a very important issue for Christians, Jews and many "pagans" in the early centuries of the Christian era. A disciplined relationship to one's body is certainly appropriate to any religion that values the material world. The rule of fasting from midnight was relaxed only in the mid–twentieth century.

Structure of the Liturgy

The primitive Eucharist probably consisted of Christianized blessing/thanksgiving prayers framing a communal meal, perhaps as in 1 Corinthians 11–14, with some form of the Liturgy of the Word following. By the middle of the second century the Eucharist achieved the basic form and structure that have endured to the present. Around 155, Justin Martyr describes the Eucharist twice in his apology to the Emperor Antoninus Pius. He first describes the Eucharist that follows baptism. His second description goes like this:

> And on the day called Sunday, all who live in the cities or in the country gather together in one place, and the memoirs of the apostles or the writings of the prophets are read, as long as time permits; when the reader has ceased, the president verbally instructs, and exhorts to the imitation of these good things.
>
> Then we all rise together and pray, and, as we said before [in the first description, with regard to the baptismal Eucharist] when our prayer is ended, bread and wine and water are brought, and the president in like manner offers prayers and thanksgivings according to his ability, and the people assent, saying Amen; and there is a distribution to each, and a participation of that over which thanks has been given, and to those who are absent a portion is sent by the deacons.
>
> And they who are well-to-do, and willing, give what each thinks fit; and what is collected is deposited with the president who succors the orphans and widows, and those who, through sickness or any other cause, are in want, and those who are in bonds, and the strangers sojourning among us, and in a word takes care of all those who are in need.[1]

Table 3.1 at the end of the chapter shows how this basic structure was filled in during the course of subsequent centuries. For now let us notice several aspects of this description.

- Readings are taken from both the Old and New Testament—for as long as time permits. Presumably, Sunday was a workday in the Roman world and the service took place before people went to work.
- The president of the assembly (who in the second century would have been a bishop) gives a homily after the readings.
- The prayers and intercessions are an important part of the liturgy. In the earlier description Justin mentions that they are concluded with the kiss of peace. Only several centuries later do we find the kiss of peace at its current location—in preparation for Holy Communion—and then only in the Roman Rite.
- The president offers prayers and thanksgivings according to his ability (more about this below).
- Holy Communion is brought to the sick and the absent. To be a Christian was to partake of the Eucharist whether you could be present for the communal assembly or not. We shall return later to the importance of this very tangible sense of Communion, both with the Lord and with one another.
- The last part of the description of the *liturgy* has to do with the collection for those who are in need. We normally don't think of this as an integral part of the Mass, but it seems rather important to Justin. It is as if he is saying that you cannot receive Holy Communion without being prepared to give what you can to those in need.

Praying and Singing

Justin says that the president (bishop) "offers prayers and thanksgivings according to his ability." Other evidence from the first three Christian centuries suggests that eucharistic prayers were not fixed formulas as much as they were prayer-structures that were filled in and extemporized by the assembly's ordained leader. (Who was ordained, how, and why does not seem to have been a major preoccupation in the very beginning.) We shall see that this changes in the fourth century. We do have several prayers that have elements going back to this period: the eucharistic prayer quoted in the third-century *Apostolic Tradition* (a kind of guide to church life) and the Prayer of the Apostles Addai and Mari from East Syria. For the most part, however, we have indications that the presider improvised the eucharistic prayer.

It is always tricky to argue from silence, but the prayers of the faithful (which one could participate in only after being baptized) and the eucharistic prayer seem to have been the only formal prayers in the liturgy. It is a fair guess to say that the early Christians sang at liturgy. Paul certainly indicates that the Corinthians did, and the New Testament is dotted with texts that look like songs, for example, the Songs of Zachariah and Mary (the well-known Benedictus and Magnificat of Luke 1), the great Christ hymns (Colossians 1; Philippians 2), and the numerous hymns in the book of Revelation. We do not, however, know precisely what they sang and when.

From Constantine to the Rise of Islam

In the year 312 the Emperor Constantine experienced something of a conversion to Christianity in the process of his military campaign to take the city of Rome. Within a few years he was master of both the Western and Eastern halves of the Roman Empire, which had been divided only about twenty years previously. This conversion (Constantine was baptized on his deathbed in 337) marked a significant moment in the history of Christian worship, as we shall see below.

Between 312 and the Muslim conquest of Jerusalem in 638 the great classic families or liturgical rites (as explained above) were formed. From a good deal of diversity in the first three centuries, this period saw a major consolidation in the structure and content of the liturgies. As the larger centers of Christian life and worship (Rome, Alexandria, Antioch, Constantinople) became more securely established, each in turn influenced diverse developments of the liturgy in their spheres of influence. Good communication existed in the Mediterranean world and so the rite experienced some cross-fertilizing as well.

Physical and Temporal Setting

The new legal status of Christianity unleashed a great building boom, in part financed by the emperor himself. Great public buildings for the Church (basilicas) as well as shrines over the tombs of the martyrs and other significant Christian sites went up everywhere. As a consequence of larger buildings and of the massive influx of new Christians the eucharistic liturgy naturally expanded in scope. Most basilicas were built on a longitudinal axis to accommodate the processions that now accompanied the liturgy. A great number of doors led into these buildings to enable large numbers of people to enter from outdoor processions through the streets, at least in major cities.

The new freedom that Christians experienced was also reflected in Constantine's decree of 321 A.D. that Sunday would be free from public business. In addition a number of feasts commemorating martyrs and other significant saints now dotted the calendar. From the fourth century on, Masses in honor of the dead became so common that the celebration of the Eucharist grew frequent—even daily. Up to the eleventh century in the West (and to this day in the Christian East) married men could be ordained as priests. But a consequence of the increased frequency of eucharistic celebration was that priests and deacons were expected to refrain from sexual relations on the nights before they celebrated the Eucharist. That is, continence (or sexual abstinence) was expected once daily Mass became the norm. And so up until the eleventh century men could marry and have children but were expected to stop having sexual relations once they were ordained.

Needless to say, the scale of the liturgy varied from place to place and day to day, but the expected norm still seems to have been the full Sunday Mass celebrated by the bishop and with a full range of ministers, including musicians.

The Structure of the Liturgy

The factors outlined above led to a filling in and more elaborate organization of the eucharistic liturgy. There is good evidence from places as diverse as Hippo in North Africa and Constantinople that in the late fourth century the liturgy began with a greeting by the presider followed immediately by the reading of Holy Scripture—no entrance rite or even opening prayer. By the middle of the fifth century, however, opening chants—mostly from the Psalms—and opening prayers began to be added in the various rites of East and West. Sometimes these chants were accompanied by litanies and processions. A common response to the litany petitions was *Kyrie eleison*—"Lord, have mercy."

As the liturgies got longer and more elaborate some of the early material such as the readings and eucharistic prayer tended to get shorter and simpler. Scripture readings were reduced from three (or even four or five) to two, usually omitting the Old Testament—at least in the West. Priests began to recite the eucharistic prayer silently. In the Eastern rites (like the Byzantine and the Syrian) many eucharistic prayers were composed and used on different days of the year. These prayers were through-composed units and evolved out of earlier prayers. By the fifth century they almost everywhere contained the following elements (not always in the same order):

- Introductory dialogue ("The Lord be with you," etc.)
- Expression of praise and thanksgiving (at times in terms of creation)
- The hymn "Holy, Holy, Holy"
- Continuation of praise and thanksgiving (at times recounting salvation history)
- The narrative of institution: "On the night he was betrayed . . ."
- A formula of memorial *(anamnesis)* and offering (that tied the institution narrative to the thanks and praise being given now)
- A petition *(epiclesis)* (for the coming of the Holy Spirit upon the eucharistic gifts and upon the assembly for its true communion)
- Intercessions for the living and the dead
- A concluding expression of praise (doxology)

Surprisingly, the institution narrative, which eventually came to be considered the center of the eucharistic prayer, can be found in only one pre–fourth-century eucharistic prayer— the one found in the *Apostolic Tradition*. (And even in that prayer we cannot be sure of the date since our manuscripts only date from the late fifth century.) The Holy, Holy, Holy (or Sanctus) is another addition to the prayers. At the risk of making a very complex development oversimplified I would suggest the following:

- The prayers of the first three centuries were improvised according to set patterns in various geographical
  locations.
- They contained short prayers of praise, thanksgiving
  and petition.
- In the fourth century the various traditions began to
  coalesce around these set patterns—to which were
  added the Holy, Holy, the institution narrative and an
  explicit *epiclesis,* or petition for the consecration of the
  bread and wine, as well as intercessions for the living
  and the dead.

Some of the eucharistic prayers of the East, like the
Anaphoras (prayers of offering) of St. Basil, St. John Chrysostom,
St. Mark and St. James, are among the most precious gems of
the Christian tradition. In the regions of what are now France,
Germany (Gallican Rite), Spain and Portugal (Mozarabic or
Visgothic Rite) such prayers were variable as in the Christian
East. These latter rites were replaced by the Roman Rite in the
course of the Middle Ages. Only the Milanese, or Ambrosian,
Rite (similar to the Roman) remains today.

In the Roman Rite only one eucharistic prayer came to be
employed: the Roman Canon, known as Eucharistic Prayer 1
today. The beginning of this prayer (the Preface—originally
meaning something declaimed aloud or "put before" in the
sense of prayed at a high voice) could be variable. The earliest
collection of Mass prayers for Rome (the so-called Verona or
Leonine [after Pope Leo the Great, 440–461] Sacramentary—a
collection of Mass booklets more than a unified sacramentary)—
has a special preface for every feast day. The Roman Canon
with its repetitions and seeming leaps of logic provides an ideal
example of the thesis that eucharistic prayers came to be made
up of units that were originally separate.

Studying the chart on the development of the western Eucharist one finds that three prayers have been added to the second-century structure at crucial points: the opening prayer, the prayer over the gifts, and the prayer after Communion. Liturgical historian Robert Taft has suggested that these were three "soft points" of the liturgy that expanded to allow for the development of more elaborate ritual—at three important processional moments: the entrance procession, the procession of the gifts and the procession for Holy Communion. In fact each of these three moments in the liturgy has the same form: an action (procession) is performed to the accompaniment of a chant and concluded with a prayer.

One can also note that the greeting of peace is placed between the common prayers (prayer of the faithful) and the presentation of the gifts in the rite described by Justin Martyr. In the Roman Rite, on the other hand, it is put between the Lord's Prayer and the reception of Holy Communion. From the fourth century on, Christians were reluctant to receive the Body and Blood of Christ. A new kind of vocabulary of awe and fear was attached to the sacred mysteries. This situation was not reversed in any significant way until the early twentieth century with the letter of Pius X urging frequent Communion.

Praying and Singing

Table 3.1 also reveals that the common prayers of the second century seem to have disappeared. Until the end of the fifth century, intercessory prayers (or what we call "the Prayer of the Faithful") followed the Gospel and homily. At first these prayers took the same form as the solemn prayers that are still used at the liturgy on Good Friday. They then took the form of litanies (consisting of short petitions followed by responses like "Lord, have mercy" or "Lord, hear us"—a more popular form coming from the Christian East and used in processions), which replaced the solemn prayers. Whatever their form, these prayers of the people disappeared after the sixth century.

We have already noted the three prayers that conclude the "soft points" of the liturgy: the opening prayer (or collect), the prayer over the gifts (or Secreta) and the prayer after Communion. Sets of these prayers began to be written down and collected from at least the middle of the sixth century. The first collection of them, misnamed the Leonine Sacramentary, was neither Leonine nor a sacramentary (a book with prayers for the priest that covered the entire year) but rather a sixth-century collection of booklets *(libelli)* of Mass prayers. Two other "families" of books arranged for the Eucharist and containing prayers for the entire liturgical year were composed for the Roman Rite. The Gelasian Sacramentary was most probably written for the titular or parish churches of Rome in the seventh century. The Gregorian Sacramentary was composed for the papal liturgy—a kind of traveling liturgy presided over by the Bishop of Rome at different churches on appropriate days. These have been called "stational" liturgies. The stations (e.g., *Statio ad S. Mariam Majorem*— Station at St. Mary Major—for the Annunciation, March 25) remained "on the books" in the Roman liturgy until the Missal of Pope Paul VI (1969).

The system of stational liturgy reveals two very important features of the Eucharist in this period. First, at the liturgy the pope would place a piece of the bread consecrated at the previous liturgy into the chalice during the fraction rite. This was a sign that there was continuity in the celebration of the Eucharist. If you will, it suggested that there was only one great eucharistic offering that the church continued to enter into at various moments. Second, at the same time that the pope was placing a fragment of the consecrated bread into the chalice, pieces of the bread consecrated at the current liturgy were being broken and placed into sacks for acolytes to carry to the churches elsewhere in the city where presbyters (priests) were celebrating the Eucharist. The latter, in turn, placed these consecrated fragments from the pope's Mass into the chalice at the time of the fraction. This practice was called the *fermentum*, which means that the local Eucharist was "brought to life" by the one major celebration of the liturgy by the city's bishop. This was another way of stressing unity by means of the Eucharist: "There is only one Eucharistic liturgy being celebrated today, and we are participating in it." We should not underestimate the power of these very tangible symbols in helping Christians understand the Eucharist as the sacrament of unity—both with the sacramental Body of Christ and with the communal Body of Christ, the Church.

Singing at the Eucharist, which consisted of unaccompanied chant, was more and more restricted to the choir (or *schola cantorum*), which consisted of men and boys. The Holy, Holy chant seems to have been an exception. The *Ordo Romanus Primus* (or "First Roman Order," a handbook of directions for a bishop's Mass, c. 700) tells us that the choir would sing all of the verses of the entrance psalm up to the point when the bishop arrived within the sanctuary and signaled to them to sing the "Glory to the Father. . ." as a way of concluding the chant. By this time the Kyrie litany had also been reduced to the singing of simply *Kyrie eleison* and *Christe eleison*, repeated as long as the pope felt necessary.

The Medieval Mass

As I mention earlier, it is somewhat misleading to encompass some one thousand years (590–1517) across the entire European continent under one title: the Middle Ages. But we can review the main lines of development. Prior to the age of mass communication, change was rather slow. Today someone could write a new liturgy and send it throughout the world over the Internet in a matter of seconds. This could not happen in a world where written communication was always done by hand—a monk or a nun painstakingly taking dictation or copying a manuscript. The relative lack of mass communication also helped the liturgy to remain somewhat local. For example, the calendars of the saints were peculiar to various cities.

In general, however, the Roman Rite was accepted everywhere in Europe—albeit with variations like the Sarum (Salisbury) Rite in England, which consisted more of local differences than a full-blown liturgical rite. The Gallican Rite in what is now France, Germany, Austria, Switzerland and the Benelux countries was displaced by the Roman Rite in the course of the eighth and ninth centuries—probably in an attempt to unify the Carolingian monarchy. Since Spain was under Muslim domination, it was not until the eleventh century that the Mozarabic or Visigothic Rite was replaced by the Roman. This rite survived only in Toledo. Its death knell was the Gregorian Reform, the consolidation of papal power under Pope Gregory VII in the late eleventh century.

Physical and Temporal Setting

Public buildings for the liturgy developed even further in the course of the Middle Ages. One of the most significant developments—since it affected both the practice and the perception of the Mass—was the placement of multiple altars in churches. This practice began in the seventh century mainly in monastic churches that wanted to imitate the liturgy of the great cities. Since it was not practical (especially in northern climates) to have processions outdoors and because most places did not have as many churches as Rome, for example, and because the custom was developing of placing the relics of the saints in altars, various altars were put inside the churches. The churches of the Christian East have never allowed more than one altar in a church, nor for that matter more than one celebration of the Eucharist on a given day. The existence of multiple altars and the practice of multiple Masses inevitably led to a certain diminishment of the sense of the Eucharist as the sacrament of unity in the Church.

In addition to adding altars some churches added chapels, sometimes located in a western apse facing the east end. The practice was most probably inspired by the veneration of relics (especially of the True Cross, whose discovery was attributed to the Emperor Constantine's mother and her pilgrimage to Jerusalem in the mid-fourth century) and was a feature of churches in the era of the first emperor of the Holy Roman Empire: Charlemagne (742–814).

Another major development was the gradual "movement" of the altar to the "east" end of the church. (This was not always the geographical east. In the early Church, however, praying toward the rising sun was an important symbol of awaiting Christ's return in glory.) There is some debate today as to whether or not the priest ever really faced the assembly during the eucharistic prayer or, if the church building had its doors to the east and apse to the west, the people turned toward the east as the priest stood at the west side of the altar to pray. Such physical orientations are somewhat difficult for us to appreciate today but they meant a great deal to premodern people. We have manuscript illuminations that show people on the "other side" of the altar while the priest prayed the eucharistic prayer. Thus the practice of the priest "having his back" to the people—facing the liturgical east—developed with the movement of the altar to the east end of the church.

Finally, the altar area in large churches became enclosed by walls and a screen, mainly to protect the monks and other clergy from the cold. The clergy were obliged to sing the Liturgy of the Hours, a series of psalms, hymns and prayers corresponding to the various times of the day, for example, Vespers in the evening. This development created what one might call a "church within a church" and can still be seen in some European countries like England and Spain as well as in Mexico.

The calendar continued to grow in the course of the Middle Ages. Almost every day now had some sort of commemoration, and the rules for distinguishing the types of celebration became extraordinarily complex. The more important feasts were equipped with octaves (celebrations that lasted eight days) but even these varied in importance. In addition, many devotional feasts, ones that did not celebrate an event or person in the history of salvation but rather some idea or aspect of faith like the Holy Trinity or the Five Wounds of Christ or the Body of the Lord *(Corpus Christi),* were added to an already packed calendar.

Structure

In the course of the eighth to the sixteenth centuries the structure of the Mass expanded at what we called above the "soft points" (or action points) of entrance procession, offertory and Communion. Often the expansion took the form of private prayers of the priest which were taken from a popular form of penitential and self-accusatory prayers called *apologiae.* Thus prayers that had been said while vesting or while approaching the altar ended up being said at the foot of the altar, especially in churches where it did not take long to process.

A series of prayers was added to the act of presenting the gifts, sometimes in the first-person singular (a sure sign of a recent addition, since traditionally the prayers of the priest had been in the plural—speaking for the whole Church). In the twelfth century the Communion of the faithful at Mass had become so rare that a ritual borrowed from the ritual of Communion of the sick, complete with penitential formulas like the confession of sins *(Confiteor)* and words of the centurion to Christ ("O Lord I am not worthy") was placed after the Communion of the priest. In addition the Fourth Lateran Council (1215) legislated the reception of Holy Communion by the faithful at least once a year. This must mean that many people were not receiving Communion at all in the course of a year, since one does not usually legislate against something that isn't happening.

The Nicene Creed was added to the celebration of Sundays and major feasts in the tenth century. It had come into the eucharistic liturgy much earlier (sixth century) in the Christian East as a way of affirming orthodoxy against heretics. In the ninth century it was adopted in the Carolingian empire and finally brought to Rome at a time when the liturgy of the city of Rome was importing texts and practices from the north.

Finally, long poetic expansions of the Alleluia verse or Gospel acclamation were introduced into the liturgy on major feast days. The most famous of these is the *Dies Irae* (Day of Wrath), which for many centuries was sung at funeral Masses but has now dropped out of the Roman Rite liturgy. Other well-known sequences include *Lauda Sion Salvatorem* (Sion, Praise Your Savior, on Corpus Christi) and *Stabat Mater Dolorosa* (Sorrowful Mother Standing [at the Cross], on Our Lady of Sorrows, September 15). The current Roman Rite has retained only these latter and two other sequences: *Victime Paschale Laudes* (Praise to the Paschal Victim—Easter) and *Veni, Sancte Spiritus* (Come, Holy Spirit—Pentecost).

Praying and Singing

A great deal happened to the conduct of the Mass in the course of the nine hundred years under consideration. In the first place the common people understood the Latin used in the liturgy less and less. We have already noted that the reception of Holy Communion became a rare event.

At the same time the estimation of the Eucharist as the real presence of the Body and Blood of Christ grew very strong. In the eleventh century the first real controversy in eucharistic theology centered around the thought of Berengar of Tours, who made a (fatal) distinction between reality and symbol in the sacrament. (In the preceding period the two words could mean the same thing.) Berengar's understanding is more "modern"—"Just a symbol." Furthermore the heresies of the Albigensians and Cathars in the twelfth century disparaged both the clergy and the real presence of Christ in the Eucharist. These are two examples of antibody movements that spring up in among Christians from time to time. They were also movements that were extremely critical of the "laxity" of the clergy. This led to a reaction not only in theology (not our focus in this chapter) but also in practice. As the sacrament was surrounded by more and more awe, people conceived an intense hunger for seeing the consecrated host. This led to a practice, beginning in the thirteenth century, of the priest elevating the host after the words: "This is my Body" in the eucharistic prayer. It also led, in the same century, to the introduction of the feast of Corpus Christi, one of the devotional feasts mentioned above.

Once the language of the Mass was no longer understood by the majority of the people (educated people of the period understood Latin) and receiving Holy Communion a rarity, it was but a short step to considering the Mass as something done primarily by the priest with others as (interested) bystanders. Mass without chanting and without an elaborate array of ministers was more and more the rule. Given the multiple altars in churches, it became possible to celebrate the Eucharist with only a server or a small number of the faithful—thus a "private" Mass. This was a far cry from the tangible signs of unity that were so important in the Roman liturgy of the fifth through eighth centuries. At the same time musical settings of the Mass and other liturgics werc bccoming more and more elaborate, beginning with the polyphonic Masses of the School of Notre Dame (Perotin, Leonin and Machaut) in the twelfth century. This movement reached a peak with the Renaissance masters like Palestrina, de Lassus, des Prez, and Victoria.

By the eleventh century the practice of using unleavened bread for the Eucharist was introduced. It was easier to reserve unleavened bread—and besides, people no longer provided the bread for their own Communion as they had in the early Church. Around the same time the custom of receiving the host on the tongue was introduced. Liturgical historian Robert Cabié suggests that the practice originated in the Communion of the sick and was adapted as a mark of respect. Receiving on the tongue also led to people receiving Communion while kneeling, as it was easier to place Communion on the tongue of someone who was kneeling. By the thirteenth century the cup was being withheld from the laity—probably on the basis of increasing concern about spilling the Precious Blood.

None of this is meant to suggest that the vast majority of Christians considered the Eucharist unimportant. On the contrary, it was immensely important and had everything to do with how medieval people viewed salvation. Having the Mass (or many Masses) offered for one's soul and/or the souls of others was a crucial part of the medieval social and cultural world. Moreover, the Mass, even if not understood, could be and was followed with great devotion—as some contemporary historians of the period, like Eamon Duffy, have insisted. On the other hand, late medieval liturgical books did not even make provision for participation by the ordinary faithful.

After the Council of Trent

The Reformation of the sixteenth century had a serious impact on the way many Christians celebrated the Eucharist. Some of the Protestant reforms retained a good deal of the medieval Mass, for example, the Lutheran rites in Sweden and parts of Germany. Some like the Reformed or Calvinist churches kept very little from the old Mass and began to celebrate it only monthly—sometimes only four times a year. Some, like the Anglicans, tended to steer a middle course but with widely varying theologies. Certain general changes took place in the course of the sixteenth-century Reformation:

- The language of the liturgy was that of the people of the region.
- The Canon of the Mass (eucharistic prayer) was abandoned because of its associations with the doctrine of sacrifice.
- Vestments, incense, candles, and so on, were abolished or left to the discretion of the local congregation.
- A table took the place of the altar.
- Most feast days were dropped; the frequency of celebration was drastically reduced.

It is often forgotten that Trent (1545–1563) was a reform council. Trent produced a number of significant doctrinal decrees that were intended to respond to the Protestant Reformers. But many Catholics recognized the need for reform *within* the Church, and one of the main reasons the council was called was to correct abuses and carry on a general reform of the Church. Trent thus undertook a major reform of liturgical and pastoral practice. For example, preaching at the liturgy was mandated for all Sundays and major feasts, special centers for the formation of priests (seminaries) were to be founded in every diocese, and the liturgical books were consolidated and edited.

In an age before instant communication such changes took time. In fact, some of Trent's reforms were not put into practice in France or the New World until one hundred years after the counci ended. Ironically, some who oppose the reforms of Vatican II appeal to Trent. The Council of Trent did not itself reform the liturgy. As at Vatican II, that was left to commissions that met after the council, which concluded its work in 1563. By 1570 the Missal of Pius V was published. It reduced the number of saints days drastically and basically adopted as a common rite one that had been used in the Roman Curia since the thirteenth century and had been popularized by the Franciscans in their missions throughout Europe. The liturgical calendar was somewhat simplified, and the number of sequences was reduced. The council itself had called for more preaching and explanation of the liturgy even as it denied (against the Reformers) that the Mass *must* be translated into the common languages. Remember that this was also a council called in reaction to the challenges posed by the Protestant Reformation. What Trent had to say about the liturgy, therefore, was not so much a complete exposition of Catholic doctrine as it was a reaction to perceived errors on the part of various Protestant Reformers.

Physical and Temporal Setting

There is little more to be said about the connection between
the liturgy and time except that by the seventeenth century,
especially under the influence of the French spirituality of the
priesthood, daily Mass was becoming the norm for every priest.
It is still encouraged in the Code of Canon Law (1983).

A significant change did take place in churches. Beginning
with the Jesuits, who had abandoned common choir, the vast
distance between the altar and the nave of the usual church
could be bridged. Renaissance and Baroque churches tend to
put their choirs into lofts, sometimes large enough to hold
small orchestras. The desire of the faithful to have visual access
to the consecrated host was thus accommodated. In addition,
tabernacles were set into the wall behind the altar such that
the altar less and less resembled a table and more and more a
throne for the Blessed Sacrament. This made sense when the
major access to the presence of Christ was by means of vision
rather than by receiving Holy Communion. As preaching
became more important, large and elaborate pulpits were
often set into the middle of the nave wall.

Structure

Nothing of major structural importance happened to the
eucharistic liturgy in the period between Trent and Vatican II.
That, of course, does not mean that nothing changed, as we
have just seen and shall now see.

Praying and Singing

Efforts to make the liturgy more participative came in the seventeenth and eighteenth centuries from quarters that may

seem odd to us—the Jansenists. We are accustomed to thinking of the Jansenists as mere moral rigorists who lead dour and severe lives. But their Christian seriousness also led them to be concerned that people participate in the liturgy with some understanding. Thus some Jansenists advocated vernacular liturgy. Others translated the Mass for the use of the faithful, but Pope Alexander VII forbade such translations late in the seventeenth century.

More fortunate were the efforts of Prosper Gueranger, a nineteenth-century Benedictine monk of Solesmes, who led the revival of Gregorian chant and of more profound understanding of the liturgy, especially with his commentary on the liturgical year. The twentieth-century liturgical movement had several sources, not least the encouragement of chant and of frequent Communion by Pius X and the liturgical weeks founded by another Benedictine, Lambert Beauduin. The liturgical movement was promoted in the United States by the Benedictines, in particular St. John's Abbey in Collegeville, Minnesota, and by a number of visionary and pioneering priests, especially in the Midwest.

Conclusion

This brings us to Vatican II and the Mass that we celebrate today. Our survey has been sweeping, and the many gaps can be filled in from the suggested readings at the end of this book. Some more historical details will inevitably inform the commentary on the Mass that follows.

Reforms were promoted even before Vatican II. A little known local council, the Synod of Pistoia (Tuscany) in 1786, anticipated many of the Vatican II reforms like the use of the people's language in the liturgy. (This was advocated as well by the first American Roman Catholic bishop, John Carroll of Baltimore, 1789–1815). Pope Pius X strongly urged Catholics to the more frequent reception of Holy Communion at the beginning of the twentieth century. By the middle of the century a movement for "dialogue Mass" had taken off in Germany and begun to spread. Pius XII relaxed the rules of fasting before Holy Communion some ten years before the Second Vatican Council.

Questions for Reflection

1. How did the space for celebrating the Mass change after Constantine and the legalization of Christianity? What difference did it make for celebrating the liturgy?
2. Which parts of the Mass tended to be cut back in the course of history? Which parts tended to expand? Why?
3. What was the *fermentum* rite? What was it meant to symbolize?

TABLE 3.1. DEVELOPMENT OF THE WESTERN EUCHARIST

Justin Martyr, c. 150	Ordo Romanus Primus, c. 700	Gallican Rite, c. 650	Medieval Roman Rite, c. 1300
Liturgy of the Word	*Liturgy of the Word*	*Liturgy of the Word*	*Liturgy of the Word*
			Private prayers
	Introit	Introit	Introit
	Kyrie	GREETING	Kyrie
	Gloria in excelsis	Trisagion	Gloria in excelsis

TABLE 3.1. Continued

Justin Martyr, c. 150	Ordo Romanus Primus, c. 700	Gallican Rite, c. 650	Medieval Roman Rite, c. 1300
GREETING	GREETING	Benedictus	GREETING
READINGS (PSALMODY?)	Opening Prayer	Opening Prayer	Opening Prayer
		OT READING	
	EPISTLE	PSALMODY	PSALMODY
	PSALMODY	NT READING	EPISTLE
			Sequence (occasionally)
		GOSP. ACCLA	Alleluia verse
HOMILY	GOSPEL	GOSPEL	GOSPEL
			Nicene Creed
COMMON PRAYERS	Dominus vobiscum/ Oremus (The Lord be with you/ Let us pray)	Litany?	Dominus vobiscum/ Oremus (The Lord be with you/ Let us pray)
PEACE			
Liturgy of the Eucharist	*Liturgy of the Eucharist*	*Liturgy of the Eucharist*	*Liturgy of the Eucharist*
PRESENTA- TION OF GIFTS	PRESENTA- TION OF GIFTS	PRESENTA- TION OF GIFTS	Preparation of Table
	Offertory Chant	Procession/ Chant	Offertory Chant

(Continued)

TABLE 3.1. **Continued**

Justin Martyr, c. 150	Ordo Romanus Primus, c. 700	Gallican Rite, c. 650	Medieval Roman Rite, c. 1300
	Prayer over the Gifts	Diptychs	Offertory Prayers
	Washing of Hands	Collect	Washing of Hands
			"Orate Fratres"
			Prayer over Gifts
		PEACE/ collect	
EUCHARIS-TIC PRAYER	EUCHARIS-TIC PRAYER	EUCHARIS-TIC PRAYER	EUCHARIS-TIC PRAYER
(FRACTION)	Lord's Prayer	FRACTION	Lord's Prayer
	FRACTION	Lord's Prayer	PEACE
COMMUNION	PEACE	Blessing/ COMMUNION	COMMUNION
	COMMUNION		Communion chant
	Communion chant	Two collects	Postcommunion collect
	Postcommunion collect		DISMISSAL
DISMISSAL	DISMISSAL	DISMISSAL	Blessing
COLLECTION			

4

The Entrance Rite

What is it that we do when we come together to celebrate the Eucharist on Sunday (for some, even more often) and how do we do it? It will take the rest of this book to answer these first questions.

The very name *church* in Greek and Latin (*ekklēsia*—to be called out, Gk.; *ecclesia*, Lat.) comes from the idea of being convoked or gathered together. Our English word comes to us from the German and is an abbreviation of the Greek *kyriakē*—what belongs to the Lord. Whatever else the Church is, it is the assembly of God's people who have been called to gather as one in the name of Jesus the Lord. The late Orthodox liturgical scholar Alexander Schmemann suggested that the procession for this assembly begins at home as people are preparing (more likely in many families that I know—rushing) to get to Church for the beginning of the Mass. Naturally this processional movement is somewhat more obvious in places where people walk to church, but writers on architecture for the liturgy point out that attention ought to be given to processional paths from parking lots so that people can "catch" the notion of journey. (I suppose that by now the phrase "the liturgy is better caught than taught" has become somewhat of a cliché, but it's nonetheless true.)

You can usually get some idea of what a particular church's eucharistic celebration is going to be like as soon as you enter the doors. If the atmosphere is hushed and the interior somewhat dark and sombre, it is probably a signal that the liturgy will be rather formal. If, on the other hand, one is greeted warmly and there is a great deal of activity in the church before the Mass begins, then chances are that the liturgy itself will have more of an upbeat feel to it. There's no use opting for one or another of these styles as preferable. I think they are strongly influenced by the local culture. The important thing to remember is that people are assembling to pray publicly as the Body of Christ.

The idea of assembling calls for a somewhat extended aside. Just who is it that is coming together to celebrate? An easy and accurate response has just been given in the previous paragraph—the Body of Christ. The Body of Christ is a difficult idea to appreciate fully today since we live in a culture that tends to emphasize the individual over the community. (This is not in any way to suggest that the modern appreciation of the individual is not an important value.) Try to think of it this way: By baptism we enter into the Church, which is Christ's Body. Sunday Eucharist is the ongoing celebration of that initiation. In the classic sequence of Christian initiation (established in the early Church and recovered in the Rite of Christian Initiation of Adults) catechesis and baptism in water are followed by a formal invocation of the Holy Spirit upon the baptized by the primary minister of the local church, the bishop, and then the newly baptized are admitted to their ultimate (and literal) incorporation into the Body of Christ—Holy Communion. Each Sunday we repeat the culmination of that process by being drawn into, incorporated, into the Body of Christ once again. So who we are as baptized Christians is a more significant issue on the scale of things than our gender, race, nationality, age, education or any other human kind of distinction you want to make. If I'm right and if you ponder this, you will realize that the consequences are quite staggering. What joins us together as faithful members of the Body of Christ is far more important than all of those normal and natural things that make us differ from one another. As we say in the Nicene Creed: "[We believe] in one baptism for the forgiveness of sins." This, it seems to me, is an extremely

---

BOX 4.1. **WHAT'S ON THE BOOKS?**

Before the Second Vatican Council the entire liturgy of the Mass could be found in one book: the Roman Missal. After the council the Missal was split into two volumes. The first is called the sacramentary, and it contains all of the prayers and directions for use by the priest. A first edition appeared in 1969, followed by a second in 1975. A third edition of the sacramentary was published by the Vatican in 2002. The significant changes from the pre–Vatican II Missal are detailed

(Continued)

BOX 4.1. **Continued**

in the following chapters. For now we can note that the number of eucharistic prayers was expanded from one to four—and then by 1975 to nine prayers. A tenth prayer—For Special Occasions—was approved for English-speaking Catholics in 1997.

The translation of the sacramentary and other liturgical books is the work of a cooperative commission of eleven bishops representing eleven major English-speaking bishops' conferences: Australia, Canada, England and Wales, India, Ireland, New Zealand, Pakistan, Philippines, Scotland, South Africa and the United States. The commission is called the International Commission for English in the Liturgy (ICEL).

The lectionary translation is prepared by each national bishops conference. For example, the English-speaking Canadian conference employs the New Revised Standard Version (NRSV) of the Bible whereas the U.S. Conference of Catholic Bishops uses the Revised New American Bible (RNAB). A new lectionary (with a five-year trial period) was published for the United States in 2001. It contains the RNAB translation of the New Testament (with some revisions) and the older NAB translation of the Old Testament. There are different approaches to the question of inclusive language, but some might have hoped that principles of inclusive language were better applied than in the present lectionary, which at times still uses male terms when men and women are meant.

Another governing text of the liturgy is the Roman calendar, which is printed in every sacramentary and lectionary. In addition to the texts from the Latin (or *typical*) edition, each national conference has its own (particular) calendar of saints and observances, for example, St. Kateri Tekakwitha—July 14—or St. Francis Xavier Cabrini—in the United States. In addition religious orders have their own particular calendars, often with different rankings of feasts. For example, in the Roman calendar July 31 is the Memorial of St. Ignatius Loyola. For Jesuits or Jesuit churches, however, July 31 is celebrated as a Solemnity.

The Directory for Masses with Children is printed in every official edition of the sacramentary. It provides some valuable suggestions when a large number of the assembly consists of young people, and I will refer to it from time to time.

Finally, each of the two books that comprise the Roman Missal has an introduction. The *General Instruction* (*Institutio Generalis*, GIRM) of the Roman Missal was presented in 2000 in advance of the third edition of the Roman Missal and now has been published in a definitive edition in the 2002 edition of the missal. A new translation of the *General Introduction to the Lectionary* (GILM) was published in 2002 and will be employed here.

I cannot emphasize enough the importance of each of these latter two documents, and I rely on them heavily in this commentary.

important consideration when it comes to issues of culture and inculturation, which are on so many people's minds today.

The General Instruction says that the elements that make up the entrance rite "have the character of a beginning, introduction, and preparation. The purpose of these rites is that the faithful who are assembling should become a community and dispose themselves to listen properly to God's word and celebrate the Eucharist worthily."[1] This, in turn, needs to be understood within the general principle for the reform of the liturgy following Vatican II: the full, conscious and active participation of the faithful which is no ecclesiastical concession but rather "their right by reason of their baptism."[2] Active participation is not an optional add-on to the Mass; it is part and parcel of what it means to express our identity as members of the Body of Christ.

It is a good idea to keep the introductory and preparatory nature of this rite in mind. It does not substitute for the Liturgy of the Word or the Liturgy of the Eucharist. Therefore, the scale of the celebration should always be kept in mind—

BOX 4.2. ENTRANCE RITE

Procession (with song)
Sign of the Cross/Greeting
(Brief Introduction)
Penitential Rite
(or Rite of Sprinkling)
"Glory to God in the Highest"
(Sundays and Feasts)
Opening Prayer (Collect)

an entrance rite that is too elaborate can dwarf the Liturgy of the Word.

The Procession

The actual entrance accompanied by a chant comes first. (There are exceptions: the funeral rite, the baptism of children within Mass and when morning or evening prayer precede Mass.) One thing that North Americans of European ancestry seem not to have mastered is the art of processing. Perhaps, as with so many aspects of formal ritual activity, processing seems a bit awkward or contrived, especially when a lone lector proceeds down the aisle followed by the priest. A procession, being like a parade and giving the impression that we are dynamic, moving somewhere—into the space of God's kingdom—needs to be somewhat more elaborate, at least when it is accompanied by singing as at the Sunday Eucharist. It is unfortunate, in my opinion, that we seem to be determined to do with as few ministers in the liturgy as possible. A good procession for a Sunday Mass would be headed by the cross of the Lord (preceded by incense if it is being used) and two servers with candles, followed by the lector(s), the deacon with the book of the Gospels and the presiding priest. A procession needs to be choreographed. It isn't a ballet but it does need to be ritualized if it is not to become sloppy and look haphazard. (One thing that I hope to convey in this book is that formal and ritual do not mean the same thing as stiff or rigid. I fear that very often people hear the latter when the former words are used. What we need more than ever today is *both* respect for our rituals *and* warmth and enthusiasm in putting them into practice.)

Only the book of the Gospels may be carried in the entrance procession. Carrying the lectionary, either by a deacon or a layperson, is explicitly excluded.[3] Perhaps the reasoning is that only the book of the Gospels has ever been decorated in a special way and shown signs of veneration. The post–Vatican II Mass designates only one place or lectern for reading the Scriptures; it is called an ambo. (Prior to Vatican II the priest read both of the readings [on the number of readings, see chapter 5] from the right [Epistle] and the left [Gospel] side of the altar—even when a lector read them from the pulpit or lectern.) The point of having only one ambo is to emphasize that Scripture is a unity for Christians—even though the Gospel has always been given a certain pride of place.

The documents prescribe a scriptural chant taken (almost always) from the Psalms as an entrance chant. Another sung text, approved by the bishops conference, may be used. It is to be "suited to the sacred action, the day, or the season."[4] How to decide what is suitable? Obviously the several criteria just mentioned come into play. At times, however, the more general criterion about the entrance rite as a way of assembling people to hear the Word and celebrate the Eucharist goes unheeded. Whatever is chosen should have the aim of bringing the assembly together—making them into an assembly. This is why, even though the entrance song might be sung alternately by choir and people or by the choir alone, it seems far more preferable to have this part of the liturgy sung in unison. Some commentators have argued that metrical hymns (rhymed stanzas that are not literally scriptural texts like "O God, Our Help in Ages Past" or "Praise to the Lord, the Almighty") have no place in the Roman liturgy. True enough: the use of metrical hymns is an innovation that came in with the Protestant Reform and blossomed in a magnificent way in the English hymnody of the seventeenth and eighteenth centuries. But hymns often succeed in molding the community into a single voice for the praise of God, and this fulfills the criterion of getting people ready to hear God's word.

The entrance procession isn't merely a functional device to get the priest from the back of the church to the front. It goes somewhere, and that somewhere is the altar. So the procession reaches a kind of conclusion with the reverencing of the altar, either merely with a bow (genuflection if the Blessed Sacrament is reserved in the sanctuary), and a kiss by the ordained ministers or also with the incensation of the altar and the cross. I have seen liturgies in which an interval of music was played while the altar was being reverenced and then the final verse of the song or hymn was sung. With talented musicians this practice can convey the importance and excitement of the world-shaking act that is beginning. Four reasons are given for the opening chant or song.[5] The opening song

- Opens the celebration
- Intensifies the unity of the assembled
- Expresses the mystery of the season or feast
- Accompanies the procession

At times one is under the impression that even if the song takes only one verse it should end if the ministers have reached their places. This approach fails especially when the hymn or song is telling a story (as many do). The chant or song is the real beginning of the Eucharist, not merely an appendage. It should enable the people to gather by praising God.

The Greeting

The first words of the presiding priest are: "In the name of the Father, and of the Son, and of the Holy Spirit," to which the people respond, "Amen." All make the sign of the cross

in the process. Fairly frequently one finds the priest beginning
with "Good Morning" or another informal greeting or even
"Let us begin in the name of . . ." Sometimes, if he's unknown
to the assembly, he introduces himself. I think that all of these
greetings are mistakes—for two reasons. The first is that the
priest sees it as his job to make people comfortable and feel
at home. "This is not a stiff occasion," he seems to be saying. "We're not here to observe fussy and ritualistic formal-
ities." It seems to me, however, that real engagement with
the mystery of God's love poured out for us in Christ is not
really accomplished by this one-sidedly horizontal approach
to the celebration. The deep joy of celebrating the Lord cru-
cified and risen can be expressed just as well by the ritual
words well done, by gesture and body language, and by the
priest actually looking at people when he is addressing them.
So we need engagement and warmth—but engagement and
warmth that respect a ritual which we all "possess" in virtue
of our baptism.

The second mistake is the priest's usurping of the role of
the community. The Mass is communal property par excellence. Introducing oneself or using informal greetings at this
crucial point puts the priest as the center in an inappropriate
way. Ralph Keifer made the astute observation in his commentary on the Mass, *To Give Thanks and Praise*, that the
Tridentine Mass put the priest at the center theologically but
made him rather anonymous ritually. The post–Vatican II
liturgy seems to have reversed this and put the priest in the
center ritually speaking.

I call this a "crucial point" in the unfolding of the celebration because I ascribe to the axiom: "Well begun is half
done." The beginning sets the tone for the entire celebration.
Therefore, whatever introductory remarks are made at this
point by the priest, deacon or lay minister need to be very

brief.[6] To borrow from Keifer once again, they need to be exhortations to prayer more than they need to be explanations. They certainly do not need to be trailers for the homily.

Act of Penitence

At this point the priest invites the assembly to participate in an act of penitence. A brief period of silence follows. In its second chapter on general elements of the Mass the General Instruction has some important observations about the value of silence.[7] it is true that moments of silence can be rather awkward, especially in cultures that are utterly inundated by sound, as modern American culture tends to be. All the more reason to cultivate a reverent silence at significant points in the celebration. This is one of those points.

It is also important to recognize that the focus of the invitation is not so much our sinfulness as it is God's compassion and mercy. Formula B, for example, reads: "Coming together as God's family, with confidence let us ask the Father's forgiveness, for he is full of gentleness and compassion." Here the emphasis is clearly where it ought to be—on God. (In a similar way we sometimes get off track in the sacrament of Penance when we think that the sacrament is more about how bad we are than about how good God is. We need a healthy consciousness of our own sinfulness—but we need to know and experience the compassion and mercy of God even more.)

Three optional types of formula follow. The first is the traditional confession of sin that was used in the Tridentine Mass by the priest and ministers at the foot of the altar. When this formula is used, it is followed by a sixfold repetition of "Lord, have mercy" and "Christ, have mercy." The second is a brief two-part verse and response. The third form, which has become most common, is a threefold invocation of Christ.

There are two things to note here. First, the invocations are always addressed directly to Christ and not to each of the members of the Holy Trinity: for example, "You were sent to heal the contrite" or "Lord Jesus, you came to reconcile us to one another and to the Father." Second, the focus is not on our sins ("for the times we have . . .") but rather on Christ as the bringer of divine mercy and healing.

The phrase "Lord, have mercy" or "Christ, have mercy" has a somewhat broader connotation than simply asking forgiveness of sins. Originally used of the Roman emperor, it meant "look favorably upon us." This is the sense in which Eastern Christians use the phrase in their litanies.

Each of the three formulas ends with an absolution, which is not the sacramental formula for penance.[8] At Easter or on any Sunday, the use of the sprinkling rite is recommended. This rite serves as a reminder of our baptism and takes the place of the act of penitence. Salt, which symbolizes freshness and protection, may be added to the water accompanied by a brief blessing.

Some have criticized the introduction of an act of penitence at this point in the liturgy. To be honest, it does seem to interrupt the flow of gathering joyfully in the Lord's name and might be better placed as a response to God's word, where for example the Episcopal Book of Common Prayer (1979) puts it. It is not likely, however, that the act of penitence will be transferred to a different point in the liturgy.

"Glory to God in the Highest"

This hymn, which follows the act of penitence on Sundays and feasts, is one of the oldest Christian poetic compositions. It is addressed both to God the Father and to God the Son. Originally used in Byzantine morning prayer as a canticle (scriptural song or poem not found in the Psalms) for morning prayer, it added solemnity to the pope's Christmas Mass in the early sixth century, and was later added to Sunday and feast-day Masses at which bishops presided. From the eighth century on it has been used at all Sunday Masses (except for Lent and Advent) and feast days regardless of the presider.

Although the instruction provides for the possibility of reciting the "Glory to God in the Highest," it seems obvious that   being a hymn   it should be sung. After all, we wouldn't dream of reciting the National Anthem. Care should be taken, however, that the musical setting of this hymn is not so elaborate or complex that it dwarfs the Liturgy of the Word which follows.

Collect (Opening Prayer)

The entrance rite is concluded with an opening prayer, technically called a collect. In surveying the history of the liturgy, we have already seen that the "soft points" of the liturgy all developed out of the same basic structure: an action, covered by a song and concluded with a prayer. The collect is a way of bringing the opening rite of the Mass to its conclusion. On Sundays in the course of the year, the opening prayer has a somewhat general character, whereas on Sundays in the major seasons or other feasts or commemorations it will usually be specific and in some way sum up the particular mystery or person being celebrated.

A word about the form of this opening prayer is in order. The instruction mandates a moment of silence after the priest has said "Let us pray." Unfortunately, this practice seems to be observed in the breach. The word "collect" can be taken in two senses. It can mean bringing the entire entrance rite to a conclusion, but it can also mean gathering up the silent prayer of the members of the assembly. The "Let us pray," then, refers not so much to the words of the opening prayer as to the unspoken prayer of the faithful. It is the job of the president of the assembly to sum up these prayers.

And so the stage is set for the community to participate in the Liturgy of the Word. It has been gathered, united in song, reflection and prayer. It should be well disposed to receive the Word of God.

Questions for Discussion

1. What is the purpose of the entrance rites of the Mass?
2. What should the act of penitence do?
3. When is the "Glory to God" used in the Mass? Is it appropriate to sing it?
4. What does "Let us pray" at the beginning of the opening prayer refer to?

Celebrating the Liturgy of the Word

We now enter into the celebration of God's word. I use the term *celebration* advisedly because we are speaking of celebration more than the mere imparting of information. The Liturgy of the Word is meant to celebrate the presence of Christ. In fact as our official documents make clear, Christ is *really* present in the assembly of the faithful, the person of the minister, the eucharistic species ("substantially and continuously") and in his word.[1] In other words, although the tradition has always given pride of place to the fact that Christ is substantially present in the consecrated bread and wine and that this presence is not something that lasts only for the duration of the celebration, at the same time there are other ways (assembly, Scripture, minister) in which Christ is truly present. Paying attention to this manifold presence of Christ has revolutionary potential in how we celebrate our liturgies.

BOX 5.1. **LITURGY OF THE WORD**

First Reading: Old Testament (or Acts of the
    Apostles Easter Season)
Responsorial Psalm
Second Reading: New Testament
Gospel Acclamation
Gospel
Homily
Profession of Faith
Prayer of the Faithful

Celebrating that presence in God's word, which the lectionary introduction calls the "today" of God's word,[2] requires something more than classroom techniques. When I ask students about the most important qualification for proclaiming the Scriptures at liturgy they often answer "the ability to read in public." On one level that's a fine answer, but the *most* important qualification is faith—really believing what is being read, namely, Christian faith.

Interestingly, the documents[3] make it quite clear that reading the Scriptures at Mass is a ministerial rather than a presidential function—the presider is to read the Gospel only when no other priest or deacon is present. Preference is given to formally instituted and other readers for the other readings.

The next chapter deals with the principles behind the construction of the lectionary as well as its content. For now we shall be concerned with the unfolding of the Liturgy of the Word. The lectionary introduction insists on the intimate connection between the Liturgy of the Word and the Liturgy of the Eucharist. They form one act of worship.[4] Renewing our appreciation for the importance of hearing Scripture proclaimed in church as well as many forms of studying the Bible more deeply is one of the greatest gifts of Vatican II. This renewal is also a wonderful consequence of the biblical and liturgical movements of the early twentieth century.

The lectionary introduction also emphasizes what we might call the aesthetic or symbolic dimension of the Liturgy of the Word. The book of the Gospels is well decorated and carried in procession. The lectionary itself is a worthily bound book, befitting the Word of God that is read from it.[5] How often have we seen people who would never dream of putting the Blood of Christ into a Styrofoam cup (except in extreme necessity) reading God's holy word from a missalette or loose sheets of paper? (These practices most often occur at occasional services like weddings when appropriate criteria for selecting lectors are not always employed.) The document also calls for an ambo (lectern) that occupies "a place in the church that is somewhat elevated, fixed, and of a suitable design and nobility. It should reflect the dignity of God's word and be a clear reminder to the people that in the Mass the table of God's word and Christ's body is placed before them."[6] The ambo is reserved for the reading and preaching of God's word, the prayer of the faithful and the *Exsultet* at the Easter Vigil. It should be a place that makes it easy for us to comprehend and appreciate the Scripture readings.

The Responsorial Psalm/Gospel Acclamation/Sequences

The psalm between the readings is called "responsorial" for two reasons. The first is the form that singing the psalm usually takes. The cantor intones the response; it is repeated by

BOX 5.2. "THE WORD OF THE LORD"

In recent years the U.S. and Canadian liturgies have changed the ending of the reading(s) before the Gospel to "The Word of the Lord" from "This is the Word of the Lord." The change was made to emphasize a point. The book from which the reading is proclaimed is not the Word of God in and of itself. The proclamation—here and now/today—is the Word of God for us.

In addition, the phrase "The Word of the Lord" also communicates slightly ambiguously the relation between the biblical word and the Word of God, who is Jesus Christ. Like the phrase at the distribution of Communion: "The Body of Christ," which can refer both to the recipient and what is received, it is important to retain this kind of rich ambiguity in the liturgy. After all, revelation for Christians is not a book. That is a mistake fundamentalists made. Revelation for Christians is primarily the personal encounter in the Church with Jesus Christ, Word of God incarnate. We believe that the canonical Scriptures faithfully reflect God in Christ and so we call them "inspired."

I fear that people who like things neat and well defined do not find this approach to liturgy very helpful. They want things to mean *this* and not *that*. But liturgy does not work that way. It's more like what the choreographer Martha Graham is supposed to have responded to a reporter who asked her to describe the meaning of a dance that her troupe had just premiered: "If I could have described it in words, darling, we wouldn't have had to dance it." To understand what she meant goes a long way toward appreciating the liturgy.

the people and then again after each verse of the psalm.[7] (The psalm may be sung directly as well—straight through by cantor, choir or the assembly.) The other reason for the terminology is that the singing acts as a kind of response by the people to God's word. It should not be forgotten, however, that the psalm is also proclamation of God's word.

There is little reason for not singing the psalm, especially at Sunday liturgies. The general introduction recommends that even if the verses cannot be sung, the people should sing the response. The official documents show great respect for the various genres that can be found in the liturgy, and of course sung poetry is one of these. To enhance the possibility of singing it is possible to choose a common psalm for an entire liturgical season, one that will be repeated week after week.[8]

When the psalm is recited (as on many weekdays) there seems to be little reason to introduce it with: "The response is . . ." After thirty-some years people know what is coming next. An appropriate period of silence between the first reading and the psalm[9] will also help people to be ready for the response.

The Gospel acclamation varies according to season. In all but Lent it is "Alleluia" repeated and with a verse intervening. As with the psalm the proper genre for the Gospel acclamation is musical. In fact the *General Introduction* says quite clearly: "The *Alleluia* or verse before the Gospel must be sung and during it all stand."[10]

The medieval liturgy contained a great number of sequences. These were poetic compositions intended to be sung and inserted before the Gospel acclamation. They were originally expansions of the alleluia. Probably the most famous of these was the *Dies Irae* (Day of Wrath) sung during the *Requiem* or Mass for the Dead and made memorable by a number of impressive musical settings like those of Mozart and Verdi. It has been dropped from the post–Vatican II liturgy. As detailed in chapter 3, only four sequences remain in the Roman liturgy and only two (for Easter and Pentecost) are mandatory.

Proclamation of the Gospel

For as long as we have had descriptions of Christian worship, the reading of the Gospel has held pride of place in the Liturgy of the Word. The *General Instruction* calls it "the highpoint of the liturgy of the word."[11] Unlike the synagogue, where the Torah (first five books of the Bible) is read first and the Prophets afterward, in the Christian church the most important reading always comes last. (For the same reason the sequence Old Testament/New Testament/Gospel is always observed in the Liturgy of the Hours, the Church's daily cycle of prayer.)

Proclaiming the Gospel may be accompanied by candles and incense. As we have seen, a special book of the Gospels, which lies on the altar for the first part of the Mass, may be used. The lectionary introduction recommends the singing of at least the opening dialogue ("The Lord be with you. . . . A Reading from the holy gospel . . .") and the concluding acclamation even if the rest of the Gospel text is spoken. We stand for the Gospel as a sign of special respect. (It would be better if people weren't asked to sit for the proclamation of the Passion on Passion/Palm Sunday and Good Friday. People who are ill or weak should always be advised that they need not stand. I think it's with good reason that someone once said: The ancient church was the church on its feet, the medieval church was the church on its knees, and the contemporary church . . . well, you can fill in the rest.)

The Homily

A homily on the readings or on one of the liturgical texts is obligatory for every Sunday and Holy Day of obligation. It may not be omitted without serious cause.[12] The lectionary introduction beautifully describes the purpose of the homily in this way: "it must always lead the community of the faithful to celebrate the Eucharist actively, 'so that they may hold fast in their lives to what they have grasped in faith.'"[13] In other words it is the job of the homily to connect what has been proclaimed with the sacramental action that follows and the expression of that sacramental action in daily life. I cannot emphasize enough the important implication of this statement. It means that there is always an intimate connection that needs to be made not only between the Scriptures and daily life or between the Scriptures and the rest of the sacramental celebration, but between the Scriptures *and* the celebration *and* daily living. This in turn implies that the sacramental celebration itself has a great deal to do with daily living—a theme to which I return in chapter 8. In short, it seems to me that the best homilies I hear make me eager to go on with the celebration of the liturgy and hopeful as well as energized about putting the Good News into practice into daily life. Or to be more accurate theologically, letting God enable me/us to put the Gospel into practice.

The Profession of Faith/Creed

In chapter 3 I noted that the Nicene Creed was introduced into the Mass in the West about four centuries after it became part of the Eastern liturgy. It was made a part of the Roman liturgy in the tenth century and remains there in the Mass for Sundays and solemnities. The new Roman Missal allows for the use of the Apostles' Creed instead of the Nicene Creed. On Easter (both the Vigil and Sunday celebrations) a dialogue form of the creed ("Do you believe . . .") is substituted for the usual method. Everyone makes a profound bow (genuflection on Christmas and Annunciation, March 25) during the words "by the power of the Holy Spirit . . . and was made man."[14]

Some commentators suggest that singing the creed is inappropriate, since we do not normally sing loyalty oaths. It has also been suggested that the creed does not really belong in the Eucharist because (1) its native home is the rites of initiation and (2) the central statement of faith at the liturgy is the eucharistic prayer.

I want to differ with both of these opinions and for several reasons. First, the creed is not a loyalty oath nor is it really an accurate and precise description of the object of our faith. The creed is a statement of praise: more oriented to glorifying God than to providing information. In this sense the creed is more like a hymn than anything else, and hymns ought to be sung. The second reason is that as much as possible needs to be done to encourage full and active participation in the celebration of the Eucharist. Having a few simple sung settings of a substantial element in the Mass like the creed can greatly enhance participation. The more that we can sing or recite together, the better. Third, it's true that the original "home" of the creed is Christian initiation. But what is earliest is not always best; some developments have been quite legitimate improvements, and I think the creed is one of them.

If there are catechumens (or "elect" in the period of Lent) in the assembly for the Liturgy of the Word, they are dismissed for further reflection on the word before the rest of us go on to profess the faith that they will join in fully at their baptism.

The Prayer of the Faithful

But some early features are indeed quite valuable. The post–Vatican II reform of the liturgy recovered one of the most important parts of the Mass—the general intercessions or prayer of the faithful. The *General Instruction*'s statement on the prayer of the faithful, to which it gives the title "universal prayer," is worth quoting in full:

> In the general intercessions or prayer of the faithful, the people respond in some way to the word of God which they have welcomed in faith and *exercising an office of their baptismal priesthood*, offer prayers to God for the salvation of all. It is desirable that such a prayer, as a rule, be included in all Masses celebrated with a congregation, so that petitions will be offered for the holy Church, for civil authorities, for those oppressed by various needs, for all people, and for the salvation of the whole world.[15]

Note that the instruction calls this prayer an exercise of the baptismal priesthood. This tells us something important about the meaning of the priesthood for disciples of Christ. It is a priestly act to pray for the world. Now priests offer sacrifice, and sacrifice of the New Testament priesthood is primarily prayer, both here and in the eucharistic prayer. The eucharistic prayer is spoken by the priest, and the people associate themselves with it actively by their acclamations and especially their "Amen." But in the general intercessions the people are active in an even more obvious way by offering the prayer themselves.

Note, too, the sequence of prayers that are offered. First for the Church, then civil authorities and then for other needs. It is a pity when the intercessions in a particular parish focus exclusively on its own needs. The celebration of the Eucharist joins us to the Church throughout the world, and there are few places more apt than the prayer of the faithful to express that explicitly. The intercessions need not be too lengthy or complex. After all, we are not informing God about something that God does not already know. There ought also to be a space for people to add their own personal needs either aloud or in silence. To formulate an entire prayer can be cumbersome. It defeats the ability of some to be extroverted and enables others to tax the patience of their coworshipers (to put it mildly). It can also lead to what I call "dueling intercessions." I can "out-intercede" you or (worse) formulate a petition that negates yours entirely. Perhaps a solution can be found by announcing a topic of intercession, for example, for the sick or those in need or those who have died, and allowing people simply to name names. (Along with some fine examples, this approach can be found in the 1979 Book of Common Prayer of the Episcopal Church.) When in doubt, the sample intercessions found in the appendix to the sacramentary are a great help. Of course the document makes it clear that the intercessions will be more focused on special occasions like weddings, baptisms and funerals.

Some care should be taken with the form of the intercessions. The priest initiates the intercessions by inviting the people to pray (in the Christian East this is done by the deacon). The invitation is not itself a prayer. The intercessions can take one of a number of forms. They can sound like the solemn prayers of the Church at the Good Friday liturgy, or (almost universal in my experience) they can take the form of a litany in which people respond with a short invocation like "Lord, hear our prayer" or "Lord, have mercy." A litany itself can take two different grammatical forms. The first (most common) is addressed to the people for their prayer: "For the

Church throughout the world, let *us* pray to the Lord." In the second the petitions are addressed directly to God: "O God for peace everywhere, we pray to *you*, O Lord."

The prayers are most aptly led by the deacon. Students often stumble when I ask them why this is the rule. The reason is quite simple. The deacon is the "ordinary minister" of the Church's interceding because he is the person who is supposed to be most clearly in touch with the world's needs. Once again we have an example of the intimate connection between the Scriptures, the Mass and daily life.

Questions for Reflection

1. Is there a difference between reading the Bible in Church and at home? What is it?
2. Is there anything particularly important about the kind of books that we read from in the liturgy?
3. Why does the reading from one of the four Gospels come last?
4. When should the responsorial psalm and the Gospel acclamation be sung?
5. What is the point of reciting the Nicene Creed during the Eucharist?
6. What is the purpose and character of the Prayer of the Faithful?

The Readings for Mass

*The treasures of the Bible are to be opened up more
lavishly, so that a richer share in God's word may be
provided for the faithful. In this way a more repre-
sentative portion of holy Scripture will be read to the
people in the course of a prescribed number of years.*

—*CONSTITUTION ON THE SACRED LITURGY*, NO. 51

With these two sentences Vatican II reversed the 1,500-
year trend of shortening the Scripture readings and
revolutionized appreciation of the Bible by Catholics. In order
to appreciate the dimensions of this change we must review
the shape of the lectionary prior to the conciliar reforms.

Prior to 1969 Scripture was read at Mass on a one-year
cycle. There were two readings at the Sunday liturgy. Readings

from the Old Testament were extremely rare. There was no
weekday cycle of readings except during Lent. On weekdays
either Sunday readings were repeated or those of the saint of
the day were used or (rather frequently at least in my youth)
those from the Mass for the Dead. The conciliar reform
changed all this.

Following a mandate in the Liturgy Constitution, the
General Introduction to the Lectionary for Mass (GILM) for-
mulated principles for the reading of Scripture in the eucharistic liturgy. I concentrate on the Sunday and feast-day readings
since they shape the experience of the majority of churchgoers. The Roman Lectionary established the pattern that has
now been followed by most churches that use a lectionary. The
result was first the Common Lectionary and now the Revised
Common Lectionary, which I return to below.

The first significant change in the 1969 Roman Lectionary
was the adoption of a three-year cycle of readings based
mainly on a (semi) continuous reading of the three Synoptic
Gospels in their traditional order:

- Year A   Matthew
- Year B   Mark
- Year C   Luke

Selections from John's Gospel are read during the great
fifty days of Easter, in Lent and at the third Mass on Christmas
Day. John 6, the Bread of Life discourse, is read for four
Sundays in the midst of the Ordinary Time B cycle since
Mark's is the shortest Gospel. The Johannine Gospels of Year
A for the third, fourth and fifth Sundays of Lent (the so-
called Scrutiny Masses—the examination and exorcism of
candidates for Easter baptism) as well as those of the Easter

season may be used in the other two when there are candidates for baptism.

The other major change in the new order of readings is
the addition of a third reading on Sundays and solemnities
(major feasts, e.g., Christmas, Easter, Ascension, Assumption).
Normally this reading is taken from the Old Testament and is
matched to the Gospel of the day by a principle that the introduction calls "harmony." The Easter season is an exception,
since there has been a long-standing tradition in the Christian
East as well as parts of the West of reading the Acts of the
Apostles during that period.

Some have found the Roman Lectionary's way of reading the Old Testament unsatisfactory. On Sundays (as
opposed to weekdays) we never get to hear the great Old
Testament narratives, for example, the stories of Genesis or
the saga of Saul, David and the kings of Israel. Put together by
an ecumenical group called the English Language Liturgical
Consultation (ELLC), the Revised Common Lectionary, used
in a number of Protestant and Anglican churches, is an effort
to address this issue. It offers the choice between "continuous" (i.e., the narratives) or "related" Old Testament readings during Ordinary Time, the thirty-four-week period
(following the baptism of the Lord and Pentecost) that makes
up the bulk of the year.

Ordinary Time, the period between the baptism of the
Lord and the beginning of Lent and after Pentecost Sunday
until the beginning of Advent (Green Sundays), has a somewhat different structure. There the second readings are always
taken from the Pauline and other letters of the New Testament.
These are unrelated (at least in principle) to the Gospel and Old
Testament readings and follow the principle of semicontinuous
reading. During the seasons of Advent, Christmas, Lent, and
Easter as well as on solemnities, the second reading is chosen

in harmony with the other two readings. In the Easter season three different New Testament books are read:

- Year A   1 Peter
- Year B   1 John
- Year C   Revelation

The weekday order of readings follows the principle of semicontinuous reading for both Scripture readings. The sequence is broken by solemnities or feasts, and special readings can be substituted in Ordinary Time for memorials of the saints and special occasions. Pastors are given latitude in rearranging the readings to make an intelligible pattern when these days interrupt the sequence.[1]

Some commentators have noted that the Sunday readings contain very few of the great stories of women like Esther or Ruth in the Old Testament. This may have been the result of unconscious prejudice but more likely is explained by the principle of the centrality of Christ (Christocentricity) that governs the Roman Lectionary and indeed all of Catholic liturgy. This is another of the issues that the Revised Common Lectionary is meant to address.

No lectionary is (or ever can be) perfect. Choices must be made when one is attempting to do justice to the proclamation of God's word. At times the choices are unfortunate, as with the lack of women's stories or the retention of Ephesians 5:21–33 on wives being submissive to their husbands. Texts like the latter can of course be dealt with in homilies that explain their context and attempt to avoid the harmful (sometimes tragic) effects of treating women like second-class citizens, but often preachers simply choose to ignore them, thus at least potentially perpetuating a cycle of oppression and even abuse.

At times preachers and others who prepare the celebration of the Church's liturgy can legitimately question why a passage began at a certain verse when another few verses might have put it into a more intelligible context. An important example of this in my opinion has a significant impact of the theology of the Mass as most people experience it. (After all, as desirable as it certainly is that Catholics read and study the Bible at other times, most Catholics will experience the Bible mainly in Church.) I refer to the second reading for Holy Thursday, the Mass of the Lord's Supper. The reading is familiar: St. Paul's account of the institution of the Eucharist in 1 Corinthians 11. The reading for Holy Thursday begins with verse 23: "For I received from the Lord what I also handed on to you, that the Lord Jesus on the night when he was betrayed took a loaf of bread . . ." Beginning the reading at this point has the unfortunate consequence of omitting the reason that Paul is talking about the institution of the Eucharist. The context of the account is the unjust assemblies of the Corinthians where some are getting drunk and stuffed while others go hungry. He boldly tells the Corinthians: "When you come together it is not really to eat the Lord's Supper." Thus, when combined with the reading of John 13, the washing of the feet, we have not so much the memorial of the introduction of a ritual or rituals for the Church as we have two "acted parables" of the meaning of the entire Passion, death and resurrection of the Lord. With good reason the Last Supper has been called the overture to the entire passion narrative. An overture states the major themes that are to follow in a musical piece. So also here, the themes of life-giving self-sacrifice and service are quite compelling. This crucial aspect of the most important three days of the liturgical year is easily missed if the proper context of Paul's account is not understood. It is of the utmost importance that we hold together the connection between Holy Scripture, the Eucharist and their moral implications in daily life.

Even with these criticisms two things need to be emphasized. First, even though we have acknowledged that the vast majority of Catholics derive their knowledge of the Scriptures from the Sunday liturgy, still it would be wonderful if more Catholics were encouraged to study the Bible outside of the liturgical context. Small Scripture discussion groups are ideal for this. Also some parishes put the readings for the next Sunday (some even the entire week) in the weekly parish bulletin. Being a Roman Catholic does not mean one has to be biblically illiterate.

Second, we started by acknowledging the importance of the Catholic recovery of Scripture in the liturgy. That point should not be lost in (relatively) minor criticism. Some people lament the loss of doctrinal and moral preaching, but the spread of the biblical readings over the three-year cycle provides ample opportunity for all of the important doctrinal and moral themes to be covered—and in the properly scriptural context of Christian faith.

The Meaning of the Liturgy of the Word

In the last two chapters we have examined the structure of the Liturgy of the Word and the Roman Lectionary of 1969. Now that the details have been attended to, we can spend some time considering the meaning of this part of the Mass. It can be summarized in three points.

First, the fundamental dynamic of the Mass, indeed of all traditional Christian liturgy, the sacraments as well as the Liturgy of the Hours, is proclamation and response. First we receive God's self-communication (here by means of the Word of God), and this receiving calls forth a response from us in terms of prayer and/or liturgical action.

This dynamic is permanent—for a basic theological reason: everything we do for the good is only a response to God's grace (self-communication). We do not even initiate our prayer by ourselves (see Ephesians 2:1–10; Romans 8:26–27). Despite the criticisms of the Protestant Reformers, the Catholic liturgy has always been (at least in its fundamental structure) firmly anti-Pelagian.

Pelagius, a theologian of the late fourth and early fifth centuries, taught that some aspects of our free will initiated our response to grace. In other words, there are ways in which we save ourselves or pull ourselves up by our own spiritual bootstraps. But Catholic doctrine, which was defended mightily on this subject by Saint Augustine, insists that our salvation is completely God's initiative. We do nothing to earn it. We can only respond. The most authentic Christian motive, therefore, is gratitude. Thanksgiving is the basis of our moral life.

This anti-Pelagianism is embodied by the structure of our Liturgy of the Word. We never baptize, witness a marriage, anoint the sick, or celebrate the Eucharist without first hearing God's word. Even the post-Vatican rite for individual penance strongly recommends a brief reading from Scripture before we confess our sins. In this way we have always acknowledged the primacy of Scripture for the transmission of Christian faith.

Second, by arranging portions of the Bible into a lectionary that has Christ and the mystery of his Passion, death and resurrection as its center, the Church has created its own biblical interpretation. To use somewhat technical terms, we have a liturgical hermeneutic (theory of interpretation) for the Holy Scriptures. At times the combination of readings will affect how one of them is interpreted. At other times, it is the liturgical feast or season that gives a special nuance to a biblical passage. For example, the responsorial psalm for Wednesday of Easter Week is Psalm 8, which contains the verse: "What is man that thou art mindful of him, and the son of man that thou dost care for him" (Psalm 8:8, RSV). Most modern translations of the Bible, recognizing the male bias in using "man" for human beings in general, change the verse either to the third-person plural or first-person plural—and rightly so. In the case of the use of this psalm in Easter week, however, the reference is to Jesus as the Son of Man. The liturgical context has changed the original meaning of the psalm.

Therefore, it is not enough to study Scripture commen taries (important and invaluable as they are). To appreciate the Scriptures as they are used at Mass one must understand their liturgical context as well.

Third, the liturgy does its work by a series of juxtapositions. (I am borrowing the term and concept from a fine book, *Holy Things*, by the American Lutheran liturgical scholar Gordon Lathrop.) The first kind of juxtaposition is found in the Bible itself. For example, Second Isaiah, in 43:18–19, recapitulates both the divine creation of the world and the world's re-creation in light of Israel's return from exile. The old is juxtaposed with the present situation to make something new. We have already seen this dynamic at work in the "today" of biblical proclamation in the liturgy (at the beginning of chapter 5). Of course, this same process is at work in the New Testament itself, which takes the Old Testament as its foundation and proclaims something new in the light of the person and work of Jesus Christ.

A second kind of juxtaposition can be found within the Liturgy of the Word itself. Traditionally the Church's eucharistic liturgy has always included more than one reading. Why? Because liturgically and homiletically a reading from Scripture can never be interpreted solely on its own. Thus the Church responds to biblical fundamentalism. The Scriptures are always to be interpreted as they "rub up against one another." Both the Bible itself and the way it is employed in the liturgy caution us against easy and simple interpretations of Christian faith.

The traditional liturgy of the Church, third, has always juxtaposed the reading of the Bible with some form of liturgical action, be it the intercessory prayers of the Divine Office, the Eucharist, baptism or some other sacrament. Thus, in a real sense the word and action (proclamation and response) play off each other, preventing another kind of fundamentalism that would be exclusively biblical or sacramental. The Word of God is always needed to interpret the sacramental rite, and the sacramental rite is needed to interpret the Word of God. And so, at least in terms of the Sunday assembly of Catholics, the Liturgy of the Word alone is not sufficient—at least ideally. (I say this somewhat cautiously since there are so many regions of the world where it is difficult to have a Sunday Eucharist because of the absence of ordained priests and at times even difficult to have Holy Communion.) Word and sacrament need each other for the full expression of Catholic faith.

Questions for Reflection

1. Why does the Church use a three-year lectionary for Sundays and major feasts?
2. Why is the Acts of the Apostles always read at the liturgy during the Easter season?
3. How does the second reading relate to the reading from the Old Testament and the reading from the Gospel during Ordinary Time?
4. Why does the Liturgy of the Word always precede the Liturgy of the Eucharist?
5. Why has the Church always used more than one reading in the Mass?

The Preparation of
the Gifts

The Liturgy of the Eucharist: Introduction

The *General Instruction* introduces the description of what we
can call the Liturgy of the Eucharist proper with the following:

> At the Last Supper Christ instituted the paschal sacrifice and
> meal. Through this meal, the sacrifice of the cross is contin-
> uously made present in the Church, whenever the priest, rep-
> resenting Christ the Lord, carries out what the Lord himself
> did and handed over to his disciples to do in his memory.
>
> For Christ took bread and the cup and gave thanks;
> he broke the bread, and gave it to his disciples saying:
> "Take, eat, and drink: this is my Body; this is the cup of
> my Blood. Do this in memory of me." Accordingly the
> Church has arranged the entire celebration of the liturgy

of the Eucharist in parts corresponding to precisely these words and actions of Christ:

1) In the preparation of the gifts, the bread and wine with water are brought to the altar, that is, the same elements that Christ took into his hands.

2) In the Eucharistic Prayer, thanks is given to God for the whole work of salvation, and the offerings of bread and wine become the Body and Blood of Christ.

3) Through the breaking of the bread and through Communion, the faithful, though they are many, receive from the one bread the Lord's Body and from the one cup the Lord's blood in the same way the Apostles received them from Christ's own hands.[1]

As we saw in chapter 2, the New Testament writers turned to the Last Supper when they wanted to describe the institution of the Eucharist, but the roots of the Eucharist in the New Testament were numerous. Certainly over the first two or three centuries the local churches throughout the Mediterranean world gradually settled on the shape to the celebration that is described in the *General Instruction*. Gregory Dix famously called it "the four-fold shape" of taking, blessing, breaking and giving. In other words, the whole of the eucharistic action from the presentation of the gifts through Holy Communion is the acting out of the pattern given by Christ at the Last Supper. Although the priest is clearly at the center of the action,[2] the instruction also emphasizes the role of the royal priesthood of the baptized, "a people called to offer God the prayers of the entire human family, a people giving thanks in Christ for the mystery of salvation by offering his sacrifice."

We shall follow a somewhat unfamiliar route in reflecting on the theological aspects of the Eucharist. Instead of talking about the meaning of subjects like Christ's real presence (transubstantiation) or how Christ acts in the Mass (the sacrifice of the Mass) and then describing how the Mass embodies these aspects, I shall start with a description of our practice and then move on to reflection. An early Christian writer (Prosper of Aquitaine, fifth century) wrote that "the rule of praying should determine the rule of believing." The shorthand way of expressing this attitude is called a *lex orandi/lex credendi* approach. In other words, the rule of the Church's prayer *(lex orandi)* has a certain priority over its rule of believing *(lex credendi)*. Practice precedes reflection. It is often said that the best catechesis, or instruction on the liturgy, is the liturgy itself. A good liturgy teaches us better than any other means—precisely because it has to be acted out (Martha Graham again) to be understood. In this way the liturgy is like a good poem. We don't decide what we want to write in concepts and then put them into poetic form. We write the poem, and the meaning evolves from the poem itself.

This present chapter describes the part of the Mass that lasts from the presentation of the gifts to the eucharistic prayer. The next chapter treats the eucharistic prayer itself. Chapter 9 is about the Communion rite and the dismissal. Chapter 10 brings all of these descriptive chapters together with theological reflection on important issues of meaning in the Eucharist: How and why do we say Christ is present? What does the Mass do? Why is it so important to relate it to our daily life? How is the eucharistic liturgy a manifestation of the Church?

Presenting the Gifts/Preparing the Altar

The Liturgy of the Eucharist proper begins with an action which in itself is quite pragmatic but through the ages has suggested a number of meanings.

BOX 7.1. **PREPARATION OF THE GIFTS**

[Altar is prepared]
Procession of the Gifts/Offertory Chant
Placement of Gifts on the Altar
Blessing Prayers/Mixture of Water with Wine/prayer
    of humility
[Incensation]
Washing of Hands
Pray, Brothers and Sisters
Prayer over the Gifts

Few points in the Mass are so controversial and liable to cause confusion as the presentation of the gifts and preparation of the altar. I have been using the terminology of the *General Instruction* (Preparation of the Gifts) rather than the traditional term *offertory* in the hope of sorting out the levels of meaning present here. The architects of the Missal of Paul VI were quite clearly concerned to transform this part of the Mass, which had in the course of time virtually become a "little Canon" or imitation of the eucharistic prayer. Some of the prayers in the pre–Vatican II Tridentine Mass were relatively recent. This is evident from their being put in the first-person singular. Consider, for example, the prayer that was said as the priest raised the host in the old offertory:

> Accept, O Holy Father, Almighty and eternal God, this spotless host, which I, your unworthy servant, offer to You, my living and true God, to atone for my numberless sins, offenses and negligences; on behalf of all here

present and likewise for all faithful Christians living and dead, that it may profit me and them as a means of salvation to life everlasting.

In this prayer the priest uses the first-person singular (I), whereas up to around the ninth century the Roman Rite always used "we/us" in the formulas of the Mass. In the first post–Vatican II revised order for Mass (called the *missa normativa* of 1965) most of the prayers were eliminated from this part of the rite. But Pope Paul VI insisted that some verbal formulas be used including the familiar invitation and response which precede the "prayer over the gifts":

Priest: Pray, brethren (brothers and sisters) that our sacrifice may be acceptable to God, the almighty Father.

People: May the Lord accept the sacrifice at your hands for the praise and glory of his name, for our good, and the good of all his Church.

Preparing the Table/Bringing the Gifts Forward

The rite begins with the preparation of the altar. Ideally the altar table should look as if it needs to be prepared. In other words, its preparation alerts us to the fact that a new part of the Mass is beginning. The altar should have only the altar cloth and nothing else on it from the beginning of the celebration. (Candles could be freestanding or placed on the altar. If there is a Gospel book, it should also be put on the altar during the Liturgy of the Word.) The sacramentary, a chalice (if it is not prepared at a side table), corporal and purificator are put on the altar table at this point. Then some members of the assembly bring forward the bread and wine for the Eucharist. The *General Instruction*[3] describes this procession with the gifts as a "praiseworthy" practice. In other words, it is desirable but not mandatory. The offering of money and gifts for the church and for the poor are appropriately brought up at this time. While the gifts are being brought forward and the altar is being prepared, we can sing an "offertory chant" taken from the Church's repertory of Latin chant or some other suitable song. This is an ideal point for a hymn that picks up on the theme of the day's Scriptures or for a choral piece if there is a choir. It's also possible to have instrumental music played at this time.

The instruction does not tells us precisely where the gifts are to be received. Presumably some flexibility is desirable here because of the variety of ways in which church buildings are arranged. In any case, there is no rule that the priest (and other ministers) must receive the gifts at the "glass wall," which seems to separate the altar area from where the assembly is located even when there is no altar rail. The gifts might be brought right up to the altar, for example.

Bread and wine are brought forward and placed on the altar. The instruction stipulates that the bread for the celebration must be made from wheat, recently baked, and unleavened. The instruction states that the bread for the celebration "truly have the appearance of food and that it is desirable for the bread to be large enough to be broken to "clearly bring out the force and importance of the sign of unity of all in the one bread and of the sign of charity, in that the one bread is distributed among brothers and sisters."[4] This of course presupposes that people will receive Communion from the bread consecrated at the present Eucharist and not from the tabernacle, as prescribed both by Vatican II and the *General Instruction*. Unfortunately, this latter directive is too rarely observed. Ignoring the directive and taking Communion from the tabernacle is a problem. It makes an unnecessary distinction between the priest and the assembly and weakens the symbolism of all offering together. It takes some planning to ensure that there is enough consecrated bread and wine for everyone, but it is not rocket science. (Of course, there are occasions when there isn't sufficient consecrated bread, but these should be exceptions rather than policy. We'll deal with Communion under both kinds in chapter 9, but for now let me offer an opinion: we will be able to tell that the Vatican II liturgical renewal has really "sunk in" when all of our churches consecrate enough bread and wine for Communion at each Mass. Why? Because then we will know "in our bones" that we really are one with Christ and with one another in this act of worship.)

A number of years ago there seemed to be some reluctance to take up a collection of money and other gifts for the poor and the church at this point in the Mass. Could it have come from some discomfort in joining the sacred and profane? As we shall see in chapter 10, combining the sacred and profane in the sense that our lives are made into "thanksgiving" is the very point of the Mass in the first place. Money is an extremely important factor in our lives. It connects us in so many ways with what we consider important: security, comfort, enjoyment, the welfare of others—especially the poor. Each congregation should explicitly earmark some part of its collection, however small, every Sunday for some worthy cause. Many churches announce where the collection will go for the current week. And so we can emphasize not only the connection between the Mass and daily life but also between the assembly as the Body of Christ and the rest of the world.

Should other gifts be brought up at this time? From time to time people want to bring gifts that are symbolic of themselves and their self-offering to the altar. There is something praiseworthy in this desire—although not when the gifts are returned! The rite does not make provision for anything other than bread, wine and money and other gifts for the church and the poor to be brought forward. This is probably a good idea. In any case only bread and wine are to be placed on the altar table.

It is wonderful to see gifts of the poor surrounding the floor next to the altar. These "fruits of creation" demonstrate that our sacramental practice is founded on the Incarnate One who took on our flesh and blood. They are symbolic of what I like to call "the tangibility of the sacred."

Whatever we offer, even and especially ourselves, it is most important to recall the fundamental dynamic of liturgy mentioned in the last chapter, namely, that nothing we do for the good in liturgy, or anywhere else for the matter, is done without the power of God's grace in Christ. We need to remember constantly the brilliant lines of one of the eucharistic prefaces for weekdays: "even our desire to thank you is itself your gift."

Placing the Gifts on the Altar/ Blessing Prayers

Next the bread and wine are placed on the altar by the priest. Frequently this part of the rite doesn't look like what's written in the sacramentary. The priest is directed to hold each of the gifts "slightly raised" above the altar and say the formula provided before he puts the paten (plate) and chalice down. So, the gifts should not be lifted up high in a gesture of offering, since strictly speaking there is only one real gesture that conveys the offering of the gifts up to God; it comes at the conclusion to the eucharistic prayer when the priest (and deacon) is instructed to lift up the gifts.

The rubrics prescribe that the priest say the blessing formulas quietly.[5] The formulas are beautiful blessing prayers modeled on the Jewish *berakah* (blessing):

> (Priest) Blessed are you, Lord, God of all creation. Through your goodness we have this bread to offer which earth has given and human hands have made. It will become for us the bread of life. (People) Blessed be God forever. (Priest) Blessed are you, Lord, God of all creation. Through your goodness we have this wine to offer, fruit of the vine and work of human hands. It will become our spiritual drink. (People) Blessed be God forever.

These prayers express a theology of blessing or acknowledging God that we will see in the next chapter underlies the theology of the eucharistic prayer. God is the true and only source of what we bring to the celebration. But the presumption in the official books is that music and/or song will continue while the gifts are being placed on the altar. The priest may even recite these prayers silently even if there is no singing or he may say them aloud. Why silently when these are such beautiful prayers? Those responsible for preparing the post–Vatican II Liturgy of the Eucharist wanted to make the eucharistic prayer stand out as clearly as possible. One way to do this was to eliminate as many spoken prayers as possible and to concentrate on the proclamation of the eucharistic prayer. This aim is defeated even further when priests ignore the rubrics and say the other

silent prayers (i.e., the formula at mixing the water with the
wine, the prayer for humility, the formula at the washing of
the hands) aloud.

Incensation

At this point another incensing of the altar is permitted. Before
this happens the priest prays privately that God be pleased with
the sacrifice we are about to offer. The incensing of the altar is
preceded by an incensation of the gifts and followed by that of
the ministers and the people. Contemporary American society
has qualms about smoke of all kinds. Incense is no exception.
This is a pity since the sweet smell of incense and especially the
sight of it rising up with our prayers is a potent image and our
liturgy is all too often image impoverished.

Washing of the Hands/
"Pray Brothers and Sisters"

The symbolic gesture of hand washing follows. At one point
many people dismissed this gesture as an outmoded practice
that originated in the practical need for the presider to wash
his hands after handling the gifts. Two facts speak against this
interpretation. First, the earliest witness we have to the practice can be found in the postbaptismal (mystagogical) homilies preached by Cyril of Jerusalem in the latter quarter of the
fourth century. He states explicitly that the priest washes his
hands as a sign of the purity needed to enter into the
eucharistic prayer.[6] Second, the presider did not necessarily
collect the gifts in the early Church. They were handled by
the deacons and other assistants who placed them on the
altar. The washing of the hands is a fine symbol of the seri-

ousness and solemnity of the great act of thanksgiving that is about to follow.

Another means of preparation is the invitation and response, "Pray, brothers and sisters . . .," which is quoted above. Here the presider enlists the assembly's aid in invoking God for the purity necessary to proclaim the eucharistic prayer. Put simply, he is saying, "Pray that I may pray this prayer well and worthily." The eucharistic sacrifice is, of course, a *verbal* sacrifice; it is not the sacrifice of sheep and goats, but rather the sacrifice of praise and thanksgiving which unites us to the self-offering of Christ, as we shall see in detail in chapter 10.

Prayer over the Gifts

The final element in this part of the rite is the second of the so-called presidential prayers of the Mass: the prayer over the gifts. This prayer functions just like the opening prayer of the Mass. It brings an action to a close, this time the procession of the gifts and preparation of the altar. As in the entrance rite the action is covered by a chant or music. In the Tridentine Missal the prayer was said silently (and called the *Secreta*, or "Secret Prayer"), but now it is said aloud. Unlike the opening prayer or prayer after Communion it is not introduced by "Let us pray," probably because the preceding dialogue had fulfilled the same purpose.

Roman Rite prayers over the gifts can be confusing. They can give the impression that the true offering of the eucharistic sacrifice has already taken place. As already has been said, there is only one true offering of the Eucharist—that in which Christ unites us to his own self-offering. So prayers like the following,

> Lord,
> look with love on our service.
> Accept the gifts we bring
> and help us grow in Christian love.
> Grant this through Christ our Lord,[7]

need to be interpreted broadly to include the whole of the Liturgy of the Eucharist. The following prayer is more suitable:

> Merciful God,
> the perfect sacrifice of Jesus Christ
> made us your people.
> In your love,
> grant peace and unity to the Church.
> We ask this through Christ our Lord.[8]

Conclusion

Although in the first four centuries the bringing of the gifts to the altar was a pragmatic and functional gesture, this part of the Mass soon took on the symbolic dimension of the offering of what we have to give so as to be united to the Lord's own self-offering. In a sense, being an "action point" of the liturgy, to use the phrase of Robert Taft, it grew like Topsy and was somewhat pruned in the post–Vatican II liturgical reform.

The preparation of the gifts is a moment in the Eucharist when we can be reminded powerfully of our need to be intentionally present—alertly and with our whole selves. This can happen best when the ritual is "choreographed" simply and with reverent attention. The we can begin to recognize the wisdom of St. Augustine, who said in a sermon to the newly baptized: "There you are on the table, and there you are in the chalice, for you are one with us."[9]

Questions for Discussion

1. Where do the prayers that begin "Blessed are you, Lord, God of all Creation" come from?
2. What should be brought forward during the preparation of the altar?
3. What is the purpose of the dialogue that begins: "Pray brothers and sisters that my sacrifice and yours . . ."?
4. Why does the priest wash his hands before the eucharistic prayer?
5. What is the purpose of the prayer over the gifts?

8

The Eucharistic Prayer

A number of years ago I was asked to respond to a survey done by several American liturgy centers preparing for a conference on Sunday Mass twenty-five years after Vatican II. Fourteen U.S. parishes were surveyed and visited several times by teams of observers. Inclusively selected people in each parish were asked questions about what they experienced immediately following a Sunday liturgy. These people were regular churchgoers, yet a large percentage of them drew a blank when it came to describing the eucharistic prayer. It's strange that what the documents call "the center and summit of the entire celebration"[1] makes such a slight impression on people, when no other aspect of the celebration calls for more comment and reflection.

The present chapter deals with (1) the general structure of the Church's collection of eucharistic prayers, (2) the essential elements that go into the makeup of a eucharistic prayer, and (3) the different eucharistic prayers currently in use in the

English-speaking world. Three new prayers were added to the traditional Roman Canon, so that there are four eucharistic prayers (I–IV). In addition, three prayers for use in Masses with children, two for Masses for reconciliation and one for special occasions have been added since 1969.

The Structure of Eucharistic Prayer

In chapter 3 I suggested that the eucharistic prayer as we know it is the result of a long period of development from improvised prayer within set structures established in the various churches of the early Christian world. During the first three Christian centuries our sources suggest that the presiding priest prayed the eucharistic prayer in extemporized fashion. It's not that he thought it up that morning while shaving. There were probably set conventions and structures for this kind of praying. In the fourth century, however, the liturgy experienced something of a revolution. After Constantine converted to Christianity (312 A.D.), the persecutions ended and thousands joined the Church, there was a greater need for structure in the liturgy. Two reasons in particular led to the writing of fixed eucharistic prayers:

1. There were a far greater number of clergy, not all of whom could be expected to have facility in constructing elaborate prayers.
2. This was the age of great controversy over sensitive doctrinal issues like the Trinity (Councils of Nicea [325] and Constantinople [381]) and the nature of Christ (Ephesus [430] and Chalcedon [451]). Sometimes differences over doctrine hinged on words or even parts of words, and so a great deal more care needed

to be given to how prayers were constructed. It was necessary that prayers conform to the orthodox faith—the faith expressed in the Nicene Creed.

But fixed prayers still allowed for some significant diversity in the structure of eucharistic prayers—a diversity that the Catholic Church recognizes today as valid and valuable in the eucharistic prayers of the Christian East, prayers that differ significantly from the Roman tradition.

Just as we can discern a general dynamic of proclamation and response that operates in every liturgy, so we can discern a similarly general pattern in every eucharistic prayer: proclamation and petition. These elements of the prayers have important technical terms attached to them: *anamnesis* and *epiclesis*, as we shall see below. But no matter how many elements we find in a particular eucharistic prayer, it will always follow this same basic pattern of proclamation *(anamnesis)* and petition *(epiclesis)*.

In the first place I am speaking of a *eucharistic* prayer, which means that it is a prayer of thanksgiving, a prayer that praises and blesses God for what has been accomplished in creation but especially in the redemption of the world, with its focus appropriately on God incarnate, Jesus Christ. Every prayer (some sooner, some later) eventually turns to petition. Let me put it in plainer words than are normally found in our current prayers: "Now, having recounted your mighty deeds of salvation, O Lord, we ask you (in full confidence that you are a God who does not go back on his promises) please make these gifts of bread and wine the Body and Blood of Christ and make us one with each other as we are made one with him for the salvation of the world."

Every eucharistic prayer has this same basic structure. Indeed, most of the great prayers of the Christian tradition, like the blessing of baptismal water or the prayers of ordination, have this structure. After all, there's a good deal of common sense here—we ask the Lord to come upon us with blessing and power because we know what kind of God the Lord is.

Each of these basic elements is expanded and given nuance in the various prayers of Christian tradition. But despite the great diversity of prayers, I believe that they can be divided into two types: proclamatory and petitionary.[2] Close examination of all the eucharistic prayers available to us shows that some prayers place the narrative of the institution of the Eucharist before they ask God to do anything. These prayers I call "proclamatory" (or *anamnetic*—for "memory"). Other prayers, like all of the current Roman Catholic eucharistic prayers, first ask God to consecrate the bread and wine (i.e., to change them into the Body and Blood of Christ) and then recount what Jesus did on the night before he died. These prayers I call "petitionary" *(epicletic)*. Each of these basic structures is perfectly acceptable because the Roman Church recognizes the great prayers like those of St. John Chrysostom and St. Basil that are used in the Byzantine tradition. These two prayers are attributed to great bishops and preachers of the late fourth century. Each prayer has the following structure:

- Thanksgiving
- Acclamation (Sanctus)
- Thanksgiving and proclamation continued
- Institution narrative
- Memorial/offering
- Petition *(epiclesis)* to change the gifts and for the unity of the Church
- Intercessions
- Doxology and Great Amen

When you compare this structure with the major elements of our Roman Catholic eucharistic prayers in the box below, you see that the petition (or *epiclesis*) is placed after the words of institution. And so these prayers I would classify as proclamatory. What difference do these various structures make? In the Middle Ages the Western (or Latin) Church tended to consider the institution narrative ("This is my Body . . .") as a moment of consecration—when the bread and wine definitively become the Body and Blood of the Lord—because at this point the Lord's own words are used. The Eastern (or Greek) Church, on the other hand, tended to consider the petition *(epiclesis)* the moment of consecration because at that point in the prayer the Holy Spirit is invoked to change the gifts—to consecrate them. To make matters even more complex and confusing, in 2002 the Catholic Church recognized the validity of an ancient eucharistic prayer from Syria that is used by the Chaldean Church, the so-called Anaphora of Addai and Mari. (Anaphora [Greek], the prayer of lifting up or offering, is the most common name given to eucharistic prayers in the East.) That prayer, used by a number of Christians especially in Iran and Iraq, is remarkable in that it has no words of institution as such. Instead, the Vatican recognized that the institution narrative is virtually present throughout the whole of this eucharistic prayer. This decision has some very important consequences for Christian faith: we should not be looking for a specific moment of consecration so much as attending to the whole prayer as a consecration (transformation) of the elements of bread and wine.

Major Elements in Eucharistic Praying

In addition to the fundamental dynamic of proclamation and petition shared by all eucharistic prayers, there are a number of different structural elements that go into their makeup. Not every tradition contains every element (as we just noted with regard to the Anaphora of Addai and Mari), and certainly not every tradition puts them in exactly the same order. Box 8.1 shows the elements in the Roman Catholic prayers in the order given in the *General Instruction*.

This order is found in every official prayer currently in use in the Roman Catholic Church with the exception of the Eucharistic Prayer I (the Roman Canon). These elements represent a rich feast of prayers in various forms of praise and petition.

1. *Thanksgiving.* The word *Eucharist* means "thanksgiving." Gratitude governs the entire prayer. Our prayer is fundamentally an acknowledgment of what God has done for us in Christ. As Christians we never thank and praise God without recognizing that Jesus Christ is the center of the divine work on our behalf and the ultimate revelation of God to us, for us, and in us.

BOX 8.1. CHIEF ELEMENTS OF THE EUCHARISTIC PRAYER

Thanksgiving
Acclamation
Petition (*epiclesis*)
Institution narrative and consecration
Memorial (*anamnesis*)
Offering
Intercessions
Final Doxology/Amen

The thanksgiving portion of the prayer is always preceded by a dialogue in which the priest as the leader of the church's prayer invites us to lift up our hearts in a chorus of praise and to give thanks to God. The greatest prayers of the Church always begin with invitation and dialogue, guaranteeing as it were that we are all on the same page.

In the Roman tradition of eucharistic praying the first part of the prayer is called a "preface." There is some debate as to the origin of the term, but it seems that *Praefatio* in Latin meant literally something that was "put before" people in the sense of being declaimed aloud. So the title *Praefatio* originally referred to the entire prayer which was proclaimed publicly and aloud—and not to an appendage pasted on to the beginning, as we refer to the preface of a book. The eucharistic prayer begins with the preface dialogue, not after the "Holy, Holy, Holy." There are currently over eighty prefaces in the collection of Roman Catholic eucharistic prayers including those in the Collection of Masses of the Blessed Virgin Mary. A few of these prefaces, like those attached to Eucharistic Prayer II and Eucharistic Prayer IV as well as the Prayers for Children, for Reconciliation and for Special Occasions, are linked in a special way with the prayers that follow. Most of the prefaces, on the other hand, can be used in combination with other eucharistic prayers. An exception is Eucharistic Prayer IV, which was composed as a unit and always has its own preface. The variability of prefaces is an opportunity for adapting the eucharistic prayer to the feast or occasion. A number have memorable lines, for example, "You have no need of our praise, yet our desire to thank you is itself your gift" (Preface for Weekdays IV) or "That you might see and love in us what you see and love in Christ" (Preface for Sundays in Ordinary Time VII).

A little known suggestion in the *Directory for Masses with Children* may be of some help in further understanding this aspect of our praying. The directory says that the presider may ask the children to voice their particular motives for thanksgiving before the dialogue.[3] One could wish that this invitation were extended at every Mass, at least to be recalled silently, so that we could be reminded that this is *our* great prayer of thanksgiving, that the gratitude we acknowledge and feel is grounded in our gratitude for what God has done in our Lord Jesus Christ. In fact, if we are truly Christian, then we attribute all of our reasons for being grateful to Christ.

2. *Acclamation.* Every eucharistic prayer contains at least three acclamations: the "Holy, Holy, Holy," the memorial acclamation and the Great Amen. Several of the eucharistic prayers for use with children provide even more acclamations on the theory that children have brief attention spans. (One could well ask if this isn't true of all of us!)

The thrice Holy or Sanctus combines two biblical verses: Isaiah 6:3 and Matthew 21:9 (see Psalm 118:26). It serves as an invitation to join the heavenly chorus in praise of God. The Sanctus serves as a reminder that we are not alone in our praise and thanksgiving. Not only do we join with Christians throughout the world at present but with angels and saints in every time and place. There is something cosmic about our Eucharist. It unites heaven and earth.

The memorial acclamation follows the account of the institution of the Eucharist at the Last Supper and draws attention to this moment as the center of the prayer. There is a choice among four different acclamations. Like the "Holy" and the Great Amen, the memorial acclamation works best when it is sung.

The final acclamation of the eucharistic prayer is the Great Amen, which brings the prayer to a conclusion glorifying God. It is the assembly's affirmation and assent to what has been voiced aloud by the priest. Like the creed, it is an act of faith that is filled with praise.

3. *Petition (epiclesis)*. The Roman tradition of eucharistic praying has always had a petition for the consecration of the gifts preceding the institution narrative. All of the eucharistic prayers in the post–Vatican II Mass have the same petition, but with a difference. All of the new prayers in the Roman Rite since Vatican II contain an explicit petition that the Holy Spirit be sent down upon the gifts. A second petition for the Holy Spirit to come upon the assembly has been placed after the institution narrative and memorial.

The *epiclesis*, whether it takes the form of an explicit request for the Holy Spirit or not, is an essential element in the eucharistic prayer, showing that we do not control the sacramental presence of the Lord but can only beg for it—albeit with complete assurance that God will be true to his promises. The petitionary character of the Roman Canon and all subsequent eucharistic prayers in the Roman Rite makes it clear that we can only participate sacramentally in Christ's presence through God's gift (grace). And so, like the anti-Pelagian character of the structure of the Mass itself (as proclamation and response), which we noted in chapter 6, the eucharistic prayer reveals the same total reliance on God's gift.

4. *Institution narrative and consecration*. The most solemn moment of the Mass takes place at this point. The Lord's own words are used, which identify the bread and wine with his Body and Blood handed over for our sake. Although we will postpone our consideration of the real presence until chapter 10, it is important to underscore the utter realism with which the Church has understood these words of Christ. The post–Vatican II liturgical reform changed the institution narrative as it had been found for centuries in the Roman Canon. The "word" over the bread now adds: "which will be

given up for you" to "this is my body." The "word" over the cup now reads: "This is the cup of my blood, the blood of the new and everlasting covenant. It will be shed for you and for all so that sins may be forgiven." This formula (and the Latin it is based on) represents a change from the old Roman Canon. The "mystery of faith" has been dropped from the Lord's word and used as an invitation to the memorial acclamation. Dissatisfaction has been voiced here and there over the translation of "all" for the *multis* (literally, "many") of the Latin text. Scripture scholars are in basic agreement, however, that in the Greek original *pollēn* suggests inclusion rather than exclusion. It is a pity that some people have such a small-minded religion that they insist only a few will be saved.

The careful reader will note that the institution narrative as we now have it does not match word for word any of the scriptural texts on which it is based. It never has. Liturgical prayer texts have never been constrained to be literal in quoting the Bible.

It is very important to emphasize that the institution narrative is part of a *prayer*. We do not stop praying when we come to the words of the Lord. Sometimes people seem to think that the words of Christ are sufficient to consecrate the bread and wine. There is an old question about the bad or mad priest who goes into a bakery and recites the consecration formula over all of the bread. If that priest, given the power of his ordination, were to say "This is my Body . . ." over the bread, wouldn't it become the Body of Christ? I have actually been asked this question several times—by people who are utterly convinced that it would. It seems to me that two considerations make that a highly doubtful position. In the first place, the tradition of the Church has always put the words of the Lord in the context of a prayer. The second reason can be discerned in the Church's theology of sacramental intention. This theory was originally developed to respond to the question of unworthy priests. Can unworthy priests celebrate valid sacraments? Yes, says the Church, as long as they are doing what the Church intends. The other side of the coin, it seems to me, is that the priest can *only* do what the Church intends. The consecration of Christ's Body and Blood takes place in the context of the Church's worship. The priest has no powers independent of that context.

5. *Memorial (anamnesis)*. As we have seen, this element of the prayer is also an apt description of the whole first part of the eucharistic prayer. It contains a very significant "therefore" (*"and so*, Father, calling to mind the death your son endured for our salvation, his glorious resurrection and ascension into heaven, and ready to greet him when he comes again . . .," Eucharistic Prayer III). The command of the Lord Jesus found in Luke's Gospel and in St. Paul's first letter to the Corinthians is a command to participate again and again in the memorial of his death and resurrection by offering this prayer and sharing in the sacred sacrificial meal. The point of the memorial is not that we are remembering the Last Supper but that we are making memorial the Passion, death, and resurrection of the Lord, which the Eucharist recapitulates in a sacramental manner. We should not neglect the eschatological note to be found here as well. Eschatology is the consideration of the end times, the completion and fulfillment of history by Christ. Our remembering also includes a looking-forward to the consummation of all things in Christ's coming in glory ("ready to greet him when he comes again"). We shall reflect more on the past-present-future dimensions of the Mass in chapter 10.

6. *Offering*. There is probably no particular aspect of the Eucharist that has been debated as much as the notion of sacrifice or offering. Who is offering what to whom—and why?

Different eucharistic prayers express this idea in diverse ways. Table 8.1 shows how the offering is expressed in the four major eucharistic prayers of the Roman Rite.

Prayer IV is unique in saying explicitly that we offer Christ's Body and Blood. When the Roman Canon was written in the fourth to fifth century the identification would not have been as explicit as the whole prayer was most probably seen as consecratory; it contains a phrase worthy of meditation: "from the many gifts you have given us, we offer . . ." In other words, offering is never something we do by our own efforts—it is always a return gift to God who has given in the first place. And so, in a real sense, all that the Christian has to

TABLE 8.1. **OFFERING IN THE EUCHARISTIC PRAYER**

EP I	EP II	EP III	EP IV
. . . and from the many gifts you have given us, we offer to you, God of glory and majesty, this holy and perfect sacrifice: the bread of life and the cup of eternal salvation.	. . . we offer you, Father, this life-giving bread, this saving cup.	. . . we offer you in thanksgiving this holy and living sacrifice.	. . . we offer you his body and blood, the acceptable sacrifice which brings salvation to the whole world.

offer is Christ himself—or to put it another way—to offer
oneself in union with Christ's self-offering for us. I hope to
show in chapter 10 that the whole point of the Eucharist is
that in it God enables us to enter into the dynamic of reciprocal gift giving, a dynamic established by God's outpouring
of the divine self in Christ.

7. *Intercessions.* Intercessions found a way into the eucharistic prayer at a fairly early stage in its development. It is as if
Christians were saying, "Even though we have interceded with
God already in the prayer of the faithful, we also want to associate our own deepest needs and desires with the holiest
moment we can conceive—the presence of Christ among us in
the eucharistic elements." With the exception of Prayer I, which
places the intercessions for the living immediately after the
"Holy, Holy, Holy," all of the prayers have intercessions that
follow upon an *epiclesis* for unity and communion. For example, Prayer III reads: "Grant that we, who are nourished by his
body and blood, may be filled with his Holy Spirit and become
one body, one spirit in Christ." There follows a plea that we
share the inheritance of the saints. The Blessed Virgin Mary and
the apostles are always mentioned in this type of formula. Then
we pray for the pope, the local bishop, the clergy, and the whole
Church as well as our particular assembly. Finally we pray for
the departed. This prayer also provides a special embolism (or
expansion) that can be used in Masses for the Dead:

> Remember our brother/sister N., whom you have called
> from this life. In baptism he/she died with Christ: may
> he/she also share his resurrection, when Christ will raise
> our mortal bodies and make them like his own in glory.
> Welcome into your kingdom all our departed brothers
> and sisters, and all who have left this world in your friend-
> ship; we hope to enjoy with them your everlasting glory,

when every tear will be wiped away. On that day we shall
see you, our God, as you are; we shall be like you and
praise you forever, through Christ our Lord, through
whom you give the world everything that is good.

This extraordinarily beautiful prayer expresses great confidence that our every tear will be wiped away and that together
with the dead we shall share in Christ's glory. One of the values of the intercessions is a reminder that our worship is not
egocentric. We join in praise with the whole world, seen and
unseen, and in pleading for the world as well. In the "Holy,
Holy" we become conscious of our solidarity with the whole
of the visible and invisible world in giving praise to our Creator
and Redeemer. In the intercessions we reaffirm our solidarity
in our earnest and fervent prayers for others: living and dead.

8. *Final doxology.* All of the eucharistic prayers end as they
began, with praise and glorification of God. Our doxology
emphasizes in a rhetorical way that Christ is the center, the
content, indeed the energy of our prayer.

The Eucharistic Prayers of the Roman Rite

As we have seen, prior to Vatican II the Roman Rite had one
eucharistic prayer, the Roman Canon, and fourteen variable
prefaces. Even during the council there were calls either for the
reworking of the Roman Canon or for new eucharistic prayers.
Pope Paul VI decided that the Roman Canon should remain
substantially unchanged but that three or four prayers be added
to the corpus. Eventually three prayers for use at Masses with
children and two prayers for Masses that have reconciliation as
a major theme were added to the stock of approved eucharistic prayers. Finally, a prayer that had been written for a Swiss
national synod in 1974 was translated into various languages

(Italian, French, German and Spanish), and English translation ultimately received approval only in the late 1990s. This prayer is called the Eucharistic Prayer for Masses for Various Needs and Occasions. All of these prayers have been printed in the same section in the Latin third edition of the Roman Missal (2002). So now we can say that we have a canon (which after all is a corpus or a collection) of ten eucharistic prayers. Many people feel that more eucharistic prayers, which would echo particular cultures, are desirable. Let us consider some of the more prominent features in the various eucharistic prayers.

Eucharistic Prayer I (The Roman Canon)

As we saw in chapter 3, the Roman Canon has a long and complex history. Its lack of logical sequence is probably a sign that it was composed of various elements at different stages. Sadly, this great monument of the Christian tradition is heard infrequently today. This is most probably because its lack of logic and its somewhat antiquated vocabulary make it difficult for people to hear easily. All the same, given its importance, it needs to be heard from time to time. Several features of the Roman Canon stand out.

- It has no preface of its own.
- Its petition to God comes immediately after the "Holy, Holy, Holy" and is repeated frequently throughout the rest of the prayer.
- It has a very local Roman flavor, honoring Roman saints like Linus, Cletus, Cecilia, Anastasia.
- It is capable of being expanded in several places—with regard both to special occasions (the newly baptized at the Easter Vigil) and to feasts (Christmas, Epiphany, etc.).

- It has a somewhat more elaborate "choreography" than the other prayers—at least with regard to the priest: a deep bow at the request that God's angel bring the eucharistic sacrifice to heaven, a sign of the cross at the word blessing in the following prayer, a striking of the breast at the words: "Though we are sinners."

Eucharistic Prayer II

This prayer was modeled loosely on an ancient prayer found in the *Apostolic Tradition*, an extremely influential set of recommendations for church order whose contents range anywhere from the late second to the mid-fourth century. That early prayer had a structure that differed significantly from the prayer that we have in the Missal. It had no "Holy, Holy, Holy" nor did it contain intercessions. Its *epiclesis* followed the institution narrative.

Our second prayer has its own preface but may be used with other variable prefaces as the occasion demands or suggests. The preface attached to the prayer focuses on the incarnation and redemption wrought by Christ. Prayer II is the shortest of all the current eucharistic prayers. According to the norms for the selection of the eucharistic prayer in chapter 7 of the *General Instruction*, its brevity makes it "particularly suitable for weekdays and special circumstances."[4] It may be used at Masses for the Dead since it has an optional embolism (expansion) in the intercession for the departed.

Eucharistic Prayer III

Like the Roman Canon, this prayer has no preface of its own and is therefore ideal for use on Sundays or feasts, especially when a seasonal preface is required, for example, Lent or Easter.

This prayer also contains some of the most memorable phrases in our current collection of eucharistic prayers. The introductory passage, which leads to the first *epiclesis,* has the lovely sentence: "From age to age you gather a people to yourself, so that from east to west a perfect offering may be made to the glory of your name" (literally, "from the rising of the sun to its setting"), derived from Malachi 1:11, the prophet's vision of the entire world offering the one God pleasing and purified worship.

Another particularly beautiful prayer can be found after the *anamnesis,* offering and second *epiclesis:* "May he (Christ) make us an everlasting gift to you and enable us to share in the inheritance of your saints, with Mary . . ." In this way the prayer picks up the very important theological idea that God's gift of self to us in Christ and particularly in his eucharistic presence naturally calls forth our own gift of self, which is still God's doing. This prayer is also especially suitable for funerals since it contains a beautiful embolism for the departed, which we quoted above.

Eucharistic Prayer IV

The last of the "ordinary" eucharistic prayers found in the sacramentary is roughly based on the model of an early Eastern Christian prayer: the Anaphora of St. Basil. This prayer is to be used as a unit, giving as it does "a fuller summary of the history of salvation."[5] Its main difference from its model can be found in the fact that it has an *epiclesis* preceding the institution narrative as in the Roman liturgical tradition.

Prayer IV is well suited to Sundays in Ordinary Time and has a wonderful and rich recounting of the work of the Lord following the "Holy, Holy." Well worth noting is the lovely phrase: "And that we might live no longer for ourselves but for him, he sent the Holy Spirit from you, Father, as his first gift to those who believe . . ." Another phrase, "he always loved those who were his own in the world," echoes the words of the Fourth Gospel (John 13:1). The second *epiclesis* has the fine image of the Holy Spirit forming us into "the one Body of Christ, a living sacrifice of praise" by our sharing in the "one bread and one cup."

Eucharistic Prayers for Use with Children I–III

In 1975 the Vatican approved three eucharistic prayers for use at Masses where there are a large number of children present. These prayers for use with children contain a number of important features, features one might even wish for in the main eucharistic prayers. In the first place they tend to be rhetorical—easy to hear. For example, the first prayer regularly repeats the phrase "God, you are wonderful." Wonder is an excellent word for the younger age group toward which this prayer is directed. The second prayer relies on the repetition of the phrase "You love us so much." The third prayer directed to early adolescence is somewhat more sophisticated and varied in its vocabulary.

The prayers provide the opportunity for multiple acclamations interspersed throughout the text. Thus they provide a good balance between the prayer that the ordained priest is deputed and empowered by the Church to pray on our behalf on the one hand and our active participation and attentiveness to the prayer, which is after all our prayer, on the other.

Eucharistic Prayers for Reconciliation I–II

Around the same time that the eucharistic prayers for Masses with children were being proposed, two other prayers were drawn up for the Holy Year 1975. Both formulas follow the

BOX 8.1. **WHAT'S A BODY TO DO?**

By its very nature liturgy is an embodied experience. It is not even that we first have thoughts and then embody them in rituals and symbols. The rituals and symbols are the very means of having the thoughts in the first place. In the words of the philosopher Paul Ricoeur, "the symbol gives rise to thought."

And so we can appreciate the significance of the use of our bodies in Christian worship. Our postures and gestures tell us as much about what we are doing as our words. In a sense our recent (forty-year-old) fascination with using our own language in the liturgy has somewhat betrayed this reality. In the last thirty-five years or so we have put what I call the choreography of the liturgy on the back burner.

So, for example, when some Catholics want to encourage active participation in the eucharistic prayer, they espouse everyone reciting the prayer together. Given the fact that one of the principal roles of the priest is to give voice to the Church's prayer, it seems that we should look elsewhere to promote active participation.

The U.S. adaptation for the Roman Rite Mass prescribes kneeling: "beginning after the singing or recitation of the *Sanctus* until after the *Amen* of the Eucharistic Prayer, except when prevented on occasion by reasons of health, lack of space, the large number of people present or some other good reason. Those who do not kneel should make a profound bow when the priest genuflects after the consecration." It goes on to add: "The faithful kneel after the *Agnus Dei* unless the diocesan bishops determines otherwise."

It may be useful at this point to consider the advantages and disadvantages of various postures. Kneeling connotes respect, reverence and adoration. It can be a powerful sign of our humility before God and our acknowledgment of the presence of the Holy One in our midst. Standing connotes freedom, independence as well as respect. In American culture polite people normally stand when someone important enters a room. Both of these postures have excellent pedigrees in Catholic worship. A number of early manuscript illustrations and ivory carvings (e.g., on book covers) show the entire assembly standing (often with arms upraised) during the eucharistic prayer. In the early Church kneeling on Sundays (along with fasting) was explicitly forbidden.

So, which is the better posture for the assembly to adopt? The answer hinges on how you think about the relation between the priest and the rest of the assembly. If one is concerned to underline the difference between them, then one will finally opt to have the assembly kneeling. If, on the other hand, one is more concerned to embody the solidarity of the baptized, then all assuming the same standing posture is more appropriate. I suspect that Catholics will continue to discuss the pros and cons of kneeling versus standing for a long time to come. Perhaps I can encourage you at this point to recall the traditional Christian adage: "In the necessary

(Continued)

BOX 8.1. Continued

---

things unity; in the unnecessary, freedom; but in all things charity."

In any case, when the assembly stands some effort needs to be made to help people assume gestures, like arms upraised (the so-called *orans* or "praying" posture), that are appropriate to manifesting reverence. This is why the rubrics propose that when everyone is standing all make a profound bow at the same time that the priest genuflects.

The first and abiding principle for the use of the body in liturgy is reverence before the God who has blessed us with such great dignity.

---

same structure of all new eucharistic prayers in the Roman Rite. Each prayer has a preface that is integral to it and is designed to be used with it.

Each of these prayers contains some memorable phrasing. For example, the preface of the first prayer reads in part:

Holy Father, compassionate and good,
it is right to give you thanks and praise,
 for you never cease to call us to a new and more abun-
     dant life.
Though we are sinners, you constantly offer us pardon
and ask us to trust in your mercy alone.

The prayer after the "Holy, Holy" is a fine expression of our confidence in the compassion of God, who does not give up on us.

Time after time, when we broke your covenants, you did
    not cast us aside;
but through the incarnation of Jesus, your Son, you bound
the human family to yourself with a new and unbreakable
    bond. When we were lost
and our hearts were far from you, you showed the depth
    of your love:
your Son, who alone is the Just One, gave himself into
    our hands
and was nailed to the wood of the cross.
Before he stretched out his arms between heaven and earth
as the lasting sign of your covenant, he desired to cele-
    brate the Passover
in the company of his disciples.

In a similar fashion the second prayer for reconciliation
proclaims God's working for reconciliation in a poetic and
rhetorically effective manner. This prayer seems more oriented
toward communal reconciliation and the search for peace and
social justice. Its preface reads in part:

In the midst of human conflict you turn our minds to
    thoughts of peace.
Your Spirit stirs our hearts, so that enemies speak again to
    each other,
adversaries join hands in friendship, and nations seek to
    live in harmony.
Through your healing power the love of peace quells
    violence,
mercy conquers hatred, and vengeance yields to forgiveness.

The same theme is picked up in the description of
Christ's work that comes after the "Holy, Holy":

> Lord of power and might, we bless you through Jesus
>   Christ, your Son,
> who comes in your name. He is the word that brings
>   salvation,
> the hand you stretch out to sinners, the way that leads to
>   your peace.
> God our Father, when we had wandered far from you,
> you called us back through your Son. You gave him over
>   to death,
> that we might turn to you again and find our way to one
>   another.

The *anamnesis* and offering formulas that follow the words of institution pick up the idea that what we have to offer comes in the first place from God—the same notion found in Eucharistic Prayer I:

> Lord our God, your Son has left us this pledge of his love.
> We celebrate, therefore, the memorial of his death and
>   resurrection,
> offering you the very gift you have given us,
> the sacrifice of perfect reconciliation.
> Father most holy,
> accept us together with your own beloved Son,
> and, through our partaking of this banquet,
> fill us with his Spirit, who heals every wound and division.

The intercessory prayer that follows the second *epiclesis* expresses in beautiful fashion the world that the Eucharist is meant to mirror:

> Lord, as you have welcomed us here to the table of your Son
> in fellowship with Mary, the virgin Mother of God,

and all the saints, so gather at the one eternal banquet
people of every race, nation, and tongue,
in that new world where the fullness of peace will reign.

These two prayers contain some of the most evocative
imagery and phrasing in the contemporary Roman Rite corpus of eucharistic praying. It would be wonderful if they were
heard more often. As the pastoral theologian Robert Hovda
once wrote: "What do you mean we need more peace liturgies? Every liturgy is a peace liturgy."

Eucharistic Prayer for Masses for
Various Needs and Occasions

The prayer for various needs and occasions was composed in
the mid-1970s for the Swiss Synod and is therefore often
referred to as the "Swiss Prayer" or the "Prayer of the Swiss
Synod." It was originally composed in French and became quite
popular. Thereafter, it was translated into Italian, Spanish,
German and finally approved several years ago for use in English.

As the directions indicate this prayer has several prefaces
(four) and corresponding sets of intercessions. Thus there are
four themes that color this prayer:

1. The Church on the Way to Unity
2. God Guides the Church on the Way to Salvation
3. Jesus, Way to the Father
4. Jesus, the Compassion of God

This prayer contains some wonderful ideas and phrases.
The continuation of the prayer after the "Holy, Holy" emphasizes the "today" of the liturgy. We are not merely recalling

something Christ did in the past, some two thousand years ago. Rather, Christ himself is at work in our midst:

> Blessed is your Son, Jesus Christ, who is present among us when his love gathers us together. As once he did for his disciples, Christ now opens the scriptures for us and breaks the bread.

In this way three of the modes of Christ's real presence that are indicated by GIRM no. 27 are represented here: Christ in the assembly, Christ in the proclamation of the word and Christ in the eucharistic elements and their sharing.

The prayer of offering that follows the *anamnesis* picks up rather well the notion that our eucharistic sacrifice is, to use the word's of the Council of Trent, a "representation of Christ's sacrifice on the Cross." We do not so much offer a new, certainly not a different, sacrifice as we enter into the one sacrifice of Christ in the "today" of the liturgy. Moreover, the second *epiclesis* connects this mode of offering with our incorporation as members of the Body of Christ, which we shall see below is such an important aspect of the meaning of the Mass:

> Until Jesus, our Savior, comes again, we proclaim the
>   work of your love,
> offering you the bread of life and the cup of blessing.
> Look with favor on the offering of your Church
> in which we show forth the paschal sacrifice of Christ
> that entrusted to us. Through the power of your Spirit
>   of love
> count us both now and for ever among the members of
>   your Son,
> whose body and blood we share.

There are many wonderful phrases in the variable prefaces and intercessions of this prayer, and I hope that they are heard often. I will single out one passage from the intercessions of the third variation (Jesus, Way to the Father), since it echoes so well the spirit and language of Vatican II's *Constitution on the Church in the Modern World* (*Gaudium et Spes,* Joy and Hope):

> Keep your Church alert in faith to the signs of the times
> and eager to accept the challenge of the gospel.
> Open our hearts to the needs of all people, so that,
> sharing their grief and anguish, their joy and hope,
> we may faithfully bring them the good news of salvation
> and advance together on the way to your kingdom.

Conclusion

In this chapter I analyzed the structure of eucharistic praying in the Church's tradition, as well as the various elements and the particular structure that characterizes the eucharistic prayer in the Roman Rite, and surveyed the ten eucharistic prayers currently approved for use in English.

I began by expressing some disappointment that the eucharistic prayer is more a high point of the liturgy in theory than it is in practice—or at least experience. Of course some of the burden for improvement rests with priests and the quality of their proclaiming and some rests with composers and musicians who create and play acclamations. But perhaps another key to enriching our experience lies with reading and praying with the texts of the liturgy just as we have discovered the importance of reading and praying with the Bible over the past forty years. At any rate, I hope that this chapter has helped you develop a deeper appreciation of the beauty and the depth of the Church's body of eucharistic prayers.

Questions for Reflection

1. Is a variety of eucharistic prayers desirable?
2. What is the basic structure of liturgical prayer? Why is it important?
3. What elements make up a eucharistic prayer?
4. Does it make a difference if the assembly participates in the eucharistic prayer?

9

The Communion Rite

The Mass is about Christ's profound desire to be one with us and about our profound desire to be one with him. Nowhere is this clearer both in word and in action than in the Communion rite. This part of the Eucharist also demonstrates how we must be joined to one another if we wish to be joined with Christ. In other words, it is about the Body of Christ in both senses of the phrase: the eucharistic Body of Christ and the Body of Christ that is the Church. Both come together in the Mass so that the venerable saying "The Church makes the Eucharist and the Eucharist makes the Church" is revealed to be true. Before we turn in the last chapter to some theological reflection, let us see how this deep union is worked out in the rites that bring the Mass to its conclusion and then send us forth into daily life.

Of the four actions (taking, blessing, breaking and giving) that have formed the structure of the Eucharist from at least the fourth century, two (breaking and giving) are found in the rites that surround the sharing of Holy Communion and the dismissal from the Mass. The rite as a whole takes the shape found in box 9.1.

The *General Instruction* describes the purpose of the Communion rite in this way:

> Since the eucharistic celebration is the paschal banquet, it is desirable that in keeping with the Lord's command the faithful who are properly disposed receive his Body and Blood as spiritual food. This is the purpose of the breaking of the bread and the other preparatory rites that lead the faithful directly to communion.[1]

In the post–Vatican II liturgy, at least in most of the United States, people who go to Mass participate in Holy Communion. The rites from the Lord's Prayer on are meant to prepare them for that act. Some people I am sure can remember the days when a priest emerged from the sacristy

---

BOX 9.1. **THE COMMUNION RITE**

Lord's Prayer
Sign of Peace
Fraction (Breaking of the Bread)
Communion
Silence/Song of Praise
Prayer after Communion
[Announcements]
Blessing
Dismissal

immediately after the consecration, went to a tabernacle, and began distributing Holy Communion as soon as the consecration was over—without any reference at all to the Communion of the Eucharist being celebrated. At times one can still see this mentality operative when Communion is taken from the hosts reserved in the tabernacle, despite the rather clear insistence of GIRM (no. 13) and the Vatican II *Constitution on the Sacred Liturgy* (no. 55) that the people "receive the Lord's body from the same sacrifice" to signify a more complete form of participation in the Mass. The instruction repeats the same idea by saying that receiving hosts consecrated at the same Mass is "most desirable."[2]

Why make a point of this? After all, it could be objected that the Body of Christ is the Body of Christ. This is true, of course. The reserved sacrament is just as much the true sacramental Body of Christ as that which is consecrated at the present Mass. What's at stake is our perception of the Eucharist as an activity in which we participate; the sign value of that participation is diminished when we habitually go to the tabernacle because it is in the mutual dividing and sharing of the *one* bread that we enter sacramentally into what Christ has done for us and is for us—God's self-giving.

The Lord's Prayer

> The Lord's Prayer is a petition for daily food, which for Christians means preeminently the eucharistic bread, and a plea for purification from sin, so that what is holy may, in fact, be given to those who are holy.[3]

In this way the *General Instruction* presents the two most common arguments given for the introduction of the Lord's Prayer into the eucharistic celebration. As early as second-century document the *Didache* Christians were encouraged to pray the Lord's Prayer three times a day, perhaps in imitation of the Jews who prayed their version of the Prayer of the Faithful (the so-called Eighteen Benedictions) three times daily. We have certain evidence of the use of the Our Father in the Mass only toward the end of the fourth century in the postbaptismal homilies of Cyril of Jerusalem. But it was not until Pope Gregory the Great (590–604) that the Lord's Prayer was placed at the end of the eucharistic prayer in the Roman Mass. Robert Taft has interpreted its introduction as owing more to the fear and awe that gripped late-fourth-century Christians as they approached Holy Communion and thinks that the petition "forgive us our sins as we forgive those who sin against us" was perceived as an appropriate way of asking forgiveness for those sins which might impede our reception of Holy Communion. The admonition "Holy things for the holy," found in almost all Eastern Christian liturgies, substantiates this insight.

Of course, the origin of a liturgical usage does not exhaust the rich variety of meanings that it can convey. We don't want to fall into the fallacy that only what is original has validity. The Lord's Prayer suggests at least five meanings—all of which enrich our approach to participating in the Body and Blood of the Lord.

1. *Hallowing the name.* Just as the rites that prepare for the eucharistic prayer look forward to it and the Church's offering, so also the prayer that immediately follows hearkens back to the sanctification of God's name that takes place in the Church's praise and thanksgiving. And so the Lord's Prayer is a way of reemphasizing that activity of praise.

2. *The Kingdom made present by desire.* The Lord's Prayer looks for the coming of God's reign into our midst. In a very real sense, as we shall see in chapter 10, that kingdom is already made present symbolically in the eucharistic banquet. The Eucharist is God's vision of what the world really ought to be about. Therefore, we pray for the coming of that Reign of God here and now in our eucharistic assembly, here and now in our world, and of course finally with the definitive coming of Christ and the end of history.

3. *Our daily bread.* Scripture scholars have found the Greek word *epiousias* (for "daily") extremely difficult to translate. It might be bread for today or perhaps bread for tomorrow. It could also mean the bread of the Kingdom. In any case, in this liturgical context we are clearly asking for the eschatological bread—*the* bread of the Kingdom—the Eucharist.

4. *Forgive us our sins.* We cannot come to the celebration of the way God wants the world to look unreconciled. We need the Lord's forgiveness even as we need to be reminded that we dare not seek that pardon without forgiving others.

5. *Save us from the time of trial.* The traditional translation of this phrase as "lead us not into temptation" can be somewhat misleading. In line with the orientation of this prayer to the end times it is more accurate to translate it as "save us from the time of trial"—in other words, save us from final damnation. The richness of this prayer is that it can sustain both of these meanings: the temptations of daily life and the need to persevere to the end despite trials.

All of these meanings combine to make the Our Father not only the best-loved Christian prayer, but also an excellent preparation for Holy Communion.

The Sign of Peace

As we saw in chapter 3 on the history of the Mass, most of the classic Christian liturgies put the greeting of peace somewhere between the end of the Liturgy of the Word and the beginning of the eucharistic prayer. The Roman Rite is an exception, placing the peace in greater proximity to receiving Holy Communion. The intent is rather clear: we need to be reconciled/at peace with our neighbor in order to participate in Holy Communion.

In many parts of the world the exchange of peace has become the part of the Mass that is engaged in most enthusiastically. It is an opportunity for the members of the assembly to express by means of gesture what is always true of Holy Communion—that being in communion with the Lord means being in communion with one another at the same time. Put it this way: there is no vertical communion (with Christ the Lord) without horizontal communion (with the Body of Christ—the Church). Moreover, the very same exchange of peace acts as a reminder, perhaps even a warning, when we are not reconciled to our neighbor that we must be in order to receive Communion with integrity.

In recent years some proposals have been made to shift the greeting and exchange of peace to the end of the Prayer of the Faithful. If this option were to be allowed, it would permit the members of the assembly more time to greet one another without unduly breaking the rhythm of the approach to Holy Communion.

As we noted earlier, Robert Hovda once said, "What do you mean we need more peace liturgies? Peace liturgies are the only kind we have." We often search for special or unusual elements in liturgy to express our duty to be just and our commitment to peace and justice when the liturgy is *always* calling us to peace and justice—if only we would pay attention.

Fraction/Breaking of the Bread

On one level the breaking of the bread is a completely practical ritual, necessary so that the consecrated body of the Lord might be shared among a number of people. This was clearly the case in the early Church when loaves of leavened bread were employed for the Eucharist. But on another level this rite is richly symbolic. Two passages from the New Testament will help us to reflect on the meaning of the fraction.

The first passage is very familiar: the supper at Emmaus on Easter Sunday evening (Luke 24:13–35). We have already dealt with this passage in chapter 2. To summarize, two disciples are walking along the road to Emmaus. They are dejected and depressed over the events of the past few days. A stranger joins them and opens up the (Old Testament) Scriptures that speak of the death and resurrection of the Lord. When they come to the village he makes as if he's going further, but they ask him to stay with them since evening has come upon them. While at supper they recognize him as he breaks the bread. That is, in this action they recognize Jesus the Risen One, whom they were certain was dead and buried. The very act of breaking bread, necessary so that food not be hoarded but shared, is the action that reveals the identity of Christ. He seems to be saying to them: "You cannot have me with you unless you recognize who I really am—the broken one in whose sharing you have true life." And neither can we appreciate the Lord's eucharistic presence without coming to the same recognition of the broken and battered One as the source of life.

The second scene is perhaps a little less familiar. It occurs in Acts 20:7–12, while Paul is having a farewell with the disciples at Troas in Asia Minor during a meeting for the breaking of the bread (clearly Luke's technical term for the Eucharist in the Acts of the Apostles) on the evening of the first day of the week. Paul speaks at length—until after midnight. The room is on an upper level of the building and has skylights. A young man named Eutychus ("Lucky") is seated on the windowsill, falls asleep and then falls out the window and down to the ground. (No doubt this is not the last time that lengthy sermonizing had similar effects in the last two thousand years.) Paul and the others go down to him. He is thought dead but Paul claims there is still life in him and goes back upstairs to break the bread. Dawn comes and Paul leaves. Meanwhile, the text says, Eutychus is taken away alive. Etienne Nodet and Justin Taylor suggest that mentioning that Eutychus has been taken away alive only after the dawning of the day and after the breaking of the bread is a subtle allusion to the fact that the Christian experiences resurrection (dawn) after the breaking of the bread in the Eucharist—in other words that the Eucharist is truly life-giving as participation in the life and presence of the Lord. Words do not capture this moment of recognition as well as the painter Caravaggio did in his *Supper at Emmaus,* which hangs in the National Gallery of Art in London. There the two disciples and Jesus are pictured in that exquisite moment of surprise and recognition as the bread is being broken. We shall return to this theme in chapter 10.

The breaking of the bread thus communicates in a symbolic way the fact that as Christians we only have life through free self-sacrifice—the brokenness of the Lord. This communication is enhanced when large eucharistic breads are used and we can see them broken. Often priests make a significant gesture at this point in the Mass. (Breaking the bread during the institution narrative is an error that confuses the sequence of taking, blessing, breaking and giving. The priest is not acting out a passion play but rather proclaiming the Church's great blessing prayer.) The use of one cup and a flagon of wine is a useful symbol. Besides not cluttering up the altar, the flagon is poured into several cups thus implying the blood of Christ poured out for us.

In chapter 3 I alluded to the practice of the *fermentum* by which presbyters in the Roman "parish" churches dropped a piece of bread consecrated at that day's papal Mass into the chalice at the time of the fraction. This commixture is a profound symbol of the unity of the Church. In the Middle Ages it also came to be interpreted as the uniting of Christ's Body and Blood as life-giving. Genuine symbols overflow with meaning, and there is no need to reduce all symbols in the liturgy to their original meaning. At times, however, this symbolic gesture was interpreted as the resurrection of the Lord who had been slain in the consecration. We shall find a way to avoid this dreadful misinterpretation of eucharistic sacrifice in chapter 10 when we consider the theology of the Eucharist.

The fraction rite is accompanied by the chanting of the "Lamb of God," which is repeated as often as it takes to conclude the rite itself.[4] This chant with its "you take away the sins of the world" is another reminder that in our participation in the Mass Christ is uniting us to the work of salvation.

Communion

If the eucharistic prayer is theologically the high point of the Mass, then certainly Holy Communion is the high point in terms of participation. This part of the rite is similar in structure to the entrance rite and the preparation of the gifts in that it includes an action (the Communion procession) accompanied by a song (the Communion chant) and concluded by a prayer (the prayer after Communion). Of course, the act of receiving the sacramental Body and Blood of the Lord is the point of this rite. From around the twelfth century the Church has maintained that in receiving under one form Christians receive both the Body and Blood of the Lord ("concomitance"). Now that the debates of the later Middle Ages and Reformation over receiving under both kinds are long past, the Church has been able more calmly to restore the cup to all of the members of the assembly. As with Communion from bread consecrated at the present Mass, the *General Instruction* recommends the distribution of the cup, when permitted, as "most desirable" because "even by means of the signs Communion will stand out more clearly as a participation in the sacrifice actually being celebrated." The instruction goes on to say in another section:

> Holy Communion has a fuller form as a sign when it is received under both kinds. For in this manner of reception the sign of the eucharistic banquet shines forth more completely and the divine will by which the new and everlasting covenant is ratified in the Blood of the Lord is more clearly expressed, together with the relationship of the eucharistic banquet to the eschatological banquet in the Father's kingdom.[5]

Sometimes we see that a large percentage of the assembly is reluctant to receive from the cup. Perhaps the medical facts and health risks have not been adequately explained. I am told that metal chalices with alcohol in them that are wiped properly are quite safe and run no risk of spreading infection. It is probably far more risky to receive Communion after the priest has put his hand into someone's mouth—or to shake the hand of someone with a cold during the exchange of peace. But I wonder if fear of infection alone explains the reluctance to receive from the cup. Perhaps people are all too aware of the awesome symbolism that is hard to avoid in sharing a cup with someone else—especially relative strangers. Lovers share from the same cup. The act is a powerful symbol of commitment and the sharing of a common fate. This is precisely what Holy Communion commits us to. As members of the one Body of Christ, we are united by his blood in a profound bond of love and mutual service. It could be that some people unconsciously but instinctively shy away from this challenging aspect of Communion with the Lord and the members of his Body. The instruction lists the occasions on which Communion under both kinds might be given and extends almost complete freedom to diocesan bishops and national bishops conferences to establish policies on this matter.[6] "Norms for the Celebration and Reception of Holy Communion under Both Kinds in the Dioceses of the United States of America" from the United States Conference of Catholic Bishops were approved by the Vatican in the spring of 2002. These norms outline the procedures for the distribution of Communion under both kinds. It seems that such careful norms are prepared with the expectation that Communion under both kinds will become the usual Sunday practice in parish churches and other eucharistic communities.

The Communion procession is accompanied by an antiphon provided in the text of the sacramentary or by a full psalm or by "some other suitable liturgical song."[7] Since the participation of the members of the assembly is desirable at this point, it seems that responsorial singing or the repetition of short chants, as in those made familiar by the monks of the French ecumenical community of Taizé, is to be preferred to using metrical hymns during the procession. In this way people do not need to carry anything in their hands while approaching the minister to receive Holy Communion. A repertory of music suitable for the Communion procession, especially psalms and songs that emphasize the corporate dimension of partaking in the Body and Blood of the Lord, has been growing over the past thirty or so years. Such songs are clearly superior to hymns in adoration of the Blessed Sacrament, hymns that surely have their place—but not during the Communion procession. We need to focus at this point not so much on adoring the presence of Christ in his sacramental Body and Blood as on the union that he is effecting with us and with one another.

All of the documents repeatedly stress that reverence is needed in receiving Holy Communion. They stress the fact that the sacred elements are received, not taken. We shall consider this aspect of Communion as gift in chapter 10. Since the posture of standing has been adopted for receiving Communion, some lack of reverence can occasionally be noted. The usual form of reverence currently recommended is a bow before and after receiving the Body and Blood of the Lord. Some people make the sign of the cross as a reverential gesture. It is always important that the sacredness of this act be recognized bodily as well as mentally. This is the very nature of liturgy.

The Communion rite is completed by the prayer after Communion—a brief prayer that normally asks that the effects of Communion lead us to the heavenly banquet or be put into practice in our daily life. During the silent prayer after Communion some canticle of praise or thanksgiving can be sung. If there is a choir, this is an ideal time for choral music. In some churches the entire assembly remains standing until all have received Holy Communion and then all sit together for the period of silent meditation and/or music. While it is most important that people have the opportunity to pray in thanksgiving after Communion and some time should always be set aside for this prayer, standing in solidarity in the ecclesial Body of Christ with which Christ brings me into Communion is also a fine symbol.

Blessing and Dismissal

The conclusion of the Mass of the Roman Rite has always been somewhat anticlimactic and very simple. If there are parish or community announcements, this is the time for them. The blessing may take either a simple or a solemn form, depending on the day. The deacon or priest (when there is no deacon) dismisses the assembly. A reason is given for the dismissal: "so that each member goes out to do good works, while praising and blessing God."[8]

The Mass, as we have already noted, originally took its name from this dismissal *(Ite, missa est),* which we normally translate: "Go, the Mass is ended" but literally means: "Go, it is the dismissal." The fact that the Mass takes one of its most important names from the dismissal is worthy of some reflection. In a sense, the Eucharist does not exist merely for itself but rather for our becoming the Body of Christ, both individually and corporately in our daily lives. The point is not to rest content and self-satisfied with our liturgical praise and worship of God, but rather to be energized by that worship to make our lives into the spiritual sacrifice that St. Paul speaks of in Romans 12:1–2. Thinking about the meaning of the Eucharist as a whole leads us to some theological reflections described in the concluding chapter.

Questions for Reflection

1. Why is it appropriate to pray the Lord's Prayer before receiving Holy Communion?
2. What are some of the images and ideas that the "fraction rite" conjures up?
3. Why should we refrain from taking Communion from the tabernacle?
4. Has the invitation to receive Communion from the cup made a difference?
5. What does the dismissal tell us about the meaning of the Eucharist?

A Theological Reflection

As I was starting to write the first chapter of this book, I ran into one of our students in the hallway. He asked what I was working on and I told him the subject of this book. His response was revealing: "I certainly hope you're not going to spend much time on that sacrifice business. What we need is someone to write about celebration." I suggested he might want to avoid reading this book when it finally appeared, since I didn't know how to write about the Eucharist without dealing with sacrifice front and center.

I think it would be difficult if not impossible for a Catholic to participate more fully in the Mass without understanding something of the importance of eucharistic sacrifice. So, in what follows I hope to make some sense of the notion of eucharistic sacrifice and another central and "controversial" issue in the theology of the Mass: eucharistic presence. But as we have already seen in our reflection on the order of Mass, the Eucharist is so much richer than controversial issues.

In this chapter I offer a reflection on the theology of the Eucharist based on the liturgy we have surveyed. That is, we shall follow a method whereby theory follows on practice, the Church's faith in action (the *lex orandi*—the rule of praying) lays the groundwork for speculation on that faith (the *lex credendi*—the rule of believing) and leads further to Christian moral action in the world (the *lex agendi*—the rule of acting). We cannot hope to provide a full theology of the Eucharist by any means—nor anything close to a "definitive" theology—but rather *one* approach to eucharistic theology that might prove helpful for people who want to make the Mass a more significant aspect of their lives. In any case, I have often thought that theology needs to be rather modest in view of its subject matter. This is only one of many possible ways to doing eucharistic theology. Some of the suggested readings at the end of the book can lead you to a deeper appreciation of the breadth and depth of Christian thinking on this most important event of Christian worship. As with any theology, the final test of these reflections is how well they are able to affect Christian practice today.

A first and extremely important factor in any theology of the Eucharist is to recognize that the Eucharist is the completion of Christian initiation. Our common practice today of baptizing infants, introducing children to first Holy Communion around the age of seven to nine years and confirming them sometime later, often in adolescence, somewhat obscures the initiation aspect of the Mass. In large parts of the early Church, confirmation was the public affirmation by the bishop of what had necessarily (necessarily because the adult candidates were naked) taken place in private in the baptistry. The newly baptized and confirmed were then admitted to the assembly's prayers, the kiss of peace and the reception of Holy Communion. This logical progression from baptismal bath to public affirmation to participation in the eucharistic meal is lost in our contemporary arrangement of initiation where confirmation serves (at least practically speaking) as a reaffirmation of baptism and looks like the culmination of initiation since it comes so much later than first Holy Communion. We can see the original pattern much more clearly celebrated in the Rite of Christian Initiation of Adults during the Easter Vigil. But certainly an argument can be made that one cannot "get more initiated" than to be *incorporated* sacramentally speaking into the Body of Christ, which is precisely what Holy Communion does. And so one can call participation in the Eucharist the ongoing and repeatable sacrament of initiation. The dying and rising with Christ that we experience once for all in baptism on account of the self-gift of God that never needs to be repeated (the basic meaning of what we call sacramental *character*) are experienced on a frequent basis in the celebration of the Mass in which we are to grow into that priestly vocation to offer the world back to God which is ours in virtue of our baptism. The Catechism of the Catholic Church puts this succinctly in its introduction to the subject of the Eucharist:

> The holy Eucharist completes Christian initiation. Those who have been raised to the dignity of the royal priesthood by Baptism, and configured more deeply to Christ by Confirmation, participate with the whole community in the Lord's own sacrifice by means of the Eucharist.[1]

Note that at the very start the Catechism accents the fact that the entire community of the baptized participates in the eucharistic sacrifice. One of the great gains in Catholic eucharistic theology in the twentieth century was the recovery of the idea that the entire priesthood of the baptized (i.e., the whole Church) celebrates the Mass and offers the sacrifice.

A convenient and very helpful framework for our reflection on eucharistic theology is provided by a statement issued
by the Faith and Order Commission of the World Council of
Churches at Lima in 1982. Sometimes referred to as the "Lima
Document," its title is *Baptism, Eucharist, and Ministry*.[2] In
the section on the Eucharist the document outlines five different meanings:

1. Thanksgiving to the Father
2. Anamnesis, or Memorial of Christ
3. Invocation of the Holy Spirit
4. Communion of the Faithful
5. Meal of the Kingdom

These five subjects provide our framework as well. We should
also note that the Catechism of the Catholic Church deals
with much of the same subject matter under the titles: "The
Sacramental Sacrifice: Thanksgiving, Memorial, Presence,"[3]
"Paschal Banquet"[4] and "Pledge of the Glory to Come."[5]

The Eucharist as Thanksgiving to the Father

Thanksgiving provides the most commonly used name for
our liturgical celebration—and for good reason since gratitude is the foundation for Christian living as well as Christian
worship. As I suggest in chapter 1, the Eucharist is our central sacramental activity because it has so much to do with
our bodies—with their nourishment and their growth. I also
suggested that Eucharist sacramentalizes a Christian response
to the profound wound in the human condition that we call
sin as well as the human need for food that sustains our bodies and meaning that sustains our spirits. The Eucharist rep-

resents a ritual unfolding of Christ's undoing of the trapped condition of human nature (original sin) and God's ultimate "No" to the violence and envy that characterize so much of our world. In this sense Christ's sacrifice is an ironic term, an *antisacrifice*—a "No" to making scapegoats and working out our own failures, fears and incapacities on the backs of others. The contemporary thinker René Girard has done a great deal to make us aware of how important the features of violence and envy are in some of our most important stories. His thinking, especially via British theologian James Alison, has significantly informed what follows.

Contemporary Christians need to recognize the basically paradoxical and ironic nature of Christian language and therefore of Christian faith. Our belief in Jesus Christ rests on the fact that Christ overturns our normal or commonsense notions of God, justice and salvation. In chapter 1, I interpreted the great Christ hymn of Philippians 2 in terms of St. Paul's image of the second Adam who reverses the Genesis 3 narrative of the origin of sin by not grasping at being at God but rather emptying himself. This kind of reversal is crucial for understanding how Jesus reveals both God and humanity to us. Some theologians go so far as to say that the privileged revelation of God as Trinity is seen in the event of the Cross, where what to normal sight looks like disaster and failure is ultimately transformed into the source of life.[6] In other words the logical thing to do is to imagine what God is like and then see how Jesus is God. But Christian faith turns that around. It says: if you want to know what God is like, you will find him fully revealed in Christ.

If you read the teaching—and especially the parables—of Jesus closely, you will find that you are in a world turned upside down, where down-and-out sinners are welcomed back with open arms and workers who start late in the day are paid

the same as those who begin work early, where the meek
inherit the earth and the poor are given the kingdom of
heaven. So when some people argue that we would do better
without words like "sacrifice" or "king" or "Lord," I think
they fail to appreciate how utterly subversive the Christian
meaning of those words is meant to be. The lordship of Jesus
does not look anything like domination or coercion but rather
service and self-sacrificing love. Sacrifice is anything but violence. In fact it is the antidote to violence in ritual form. The
priesthood of Jesus is completely unlike the hereditary and
sacrificial priesthood of the Old Testament—as the letter to
the Hebrews makes clear. Truth be told, it takes a great deal
of imagination to do Christian theology well. Those who insist
on literalism betray Christianity at its source—the Gospels and
Christ himself. Paradox and irony can be frustrating but anything less is untrue to the Triune God, who always defies our
attempts to put "him" into our human structures and categories even as "he" completely and irrevocably commits himself to us. I'm not saying you need a Ph.D. to have Christian
faith, but you do have to be able to tolerate some ambiguity
and nuance.

Flannery O'Connor is famous for having written to a
friend about the Eucharist: "If it's only a symbol, then to hell
with it." Any Catholic can appreciate what she was trying to
express. Catholics (and in fact all traditional Christian theologies) affirm the real presence of the Lord in the consecrated bread and wine. Her use of the word *symbol*, however,
was unfortunate, since it is only in the realm of symbol and
ritual that we are able to talk about God and worship as
Christians. Late-twentieth-century Catholic theology, especially in the work of the Dominican Edward Schillebeeckx and
the Jesuit Karl Rahner, saw the whole notion of sacrament as
related to both Christ and to the Church. Sacrament is not a

term that can only be applied to seven ritual moments and activities of the Christian life. Just as Christ is the symbol or sacrament of God in the sense of self-expression, so the Church is a sacrament of Christ. The seven sacraments of the Church are the symbols of both Christ and the Church that are employed in the various situations of life. I summarize this by a brief definition of sacrament in an attempt to capture their dynamic nature—the fact that they are primarily activities, not things.

Since the Eucharist *is* Jesus and *is* his saving activity, then it must take on the contours of the Gospel itself. Note that I did not write "is about Jesus" but rather "is Jesus." The point of the Mass is not insight or information but rather encounter and transformation. As my late and much missed colleague Joseph Powers, S.J., used to say: "The transformation in question is most of all our transformation." I would put it this way—we speak of the transformation of the gifts of bread and wine into the Body and Blood of Christ so that ultimately we are transformed into the Body and Blood of Christ for the world. That is why the great St. Augustine was able to tell his hearers in Hippo: "There is your mystery on the table. Be

---

BOX 10.1. **A DEFINITION OF SACRAMENT**

Sacraments are symbolic/ritual activities that effectively mediate Christian identity by re-actualizing the Paschal Mystery (Passion, death and resurrection of Jesus Christ) in the context of the Church as his Body and in the power of the Holy Spirit.

what you receive."[7] In other words, we need to think of Communion *both* as our receiving the living Lord *and* as the Body of Christ incorporating us. We receive Christ into our bodies and Christ receives us into his body—the Church, which is his sacrament in the world.

Since the Eucharist is the presence among us of Christ's saving activity, it must somehow recapitulate Jesus and his activity in a ritual way. That is why I call my approach a "ritual action" theory of eucharistic theology. I do not mean "ritualistic," of course. Christian liturgy is not "hocus-pocus." That phrase was actually coined during the Middle Ages as a mock on the "Hoc est enim corpus meum" of the institution narrative—as if the central words of the Mass were magic. But they are not magic. There is no Christian ritual without the Word of God and faith. Given the necessary juxtaposition of word and action spoken of earlier, we can find the Christian reversal—this irony and paradox—in ritual form in the playing out of the eucharistic liturgy itself. So we can find our communal and individual entry into this experience of the Paschal Mystery, the Passion, death and resurrection of the Lord, in the very pattern of the Eucharist. The pattern itself is, however, not sufficient as we shall see below. It can never substitute for faith expressed in the petition for the Holy Spirit to enliven our offering: liturgy is always God's act first.

As we saw in chapter 2, in reflecting on Jewish meals and Jewish prayer, thanksgiving is best understood under the umbrella of "acknowledgment." The Christian (the human being as God intended) is the one who completely and thoroughly acknowledges God as the source of creation and redemption, who in blessing God is able to recognize all of God's blessings. The true human (Jesus, the second Adam as opposed to the first Adam) is the one who does not put himself or herself in the place of God, does not grasp at being like

God, but acknowledges his or her creaturehood. Another profound irony is at work here: Jesus reveals true humanity at the same time as he embodies divinity: self-emptying. Note that this is not an image of God that we could arrive at without the revelation of the Triune God on the Cross.

Therefore, thanksgiving sums up the Christian *berakah* (blessing)—total acknowledgment of God. It is played out ritually by our bringing the gifts of creation to the Lord's table and verbally by our expression of thanks in the main verb that governs our eucharistic praying: "It is right and just always and everywhere to give you thanks." The Lima Document puts it beautifully:

> The eucharist thus signifies what the world is to become: an offering and hymn of praise to the Creator, a universal communion in the body of Christ, a kingdom of justice, love and peace in the Holy Spirit.[8]

This is why the Catechism can call the Eucharist "the sum and summary of our faith."[9] And so the notion that governs the eucharistic prayer is thanksgiving for the gift that God has given in Christ—God's own self. In Christian theology this gift has been called grace. The gift character of the Eucharist sets up a dynamic that calls forth our own response in the offering of the Eucharist. Remember the phrase from Eucharistic Prayer I—"we offer you from what you have given us" and its "cousin" from the Liturgy of St. John Chrysostom: "We offer you your own from your own." We can only offer because God has offered first. As Chauvet pointed out brilliantly, God's gift does not attain its true character as gift until it is received. This does not mean that the gift is not real or objective. We have traditionally referred to the *ex opere operato* character of the sacrament, meaning that it "works" because it is a sacrament, correctly celebrated according to the intention of the Church, not because of the subjective belief of the believer or the worthiness of the minister. At the same time any sacrament is incomplete without our own reception in faith and love. The Eucharist is our primary ritual example of this reciprocal dynamic of the Christian life. Loius-Marie Chauvet has also shown that our verbal offering in the eucharistic prayer is empty unless we put "flesh" on the "bones" of that offering by the way we live our lives. For him sacrament is the indispensable broker of Christian identity—a broker between the Scriptures and ethics (Christian living). Thus Christian identity rests on the tripod of Scripture, Sacrament and Ethics—all of which need to be balanced—and the tripod corresponds to the classic triad of the Greeks: Truth, Beauty and Goodness. Sacrament and liturgy are the prime expression of the beautiful in the Christian life and we have an unbalanced Christianity when we neglect them.

The Christian life is characterized above all by gratitude for salvation. Saved from what? The vicious circle created by sin in which we increase our violence and rapacity even as we try on our own to achieve significance—grasp at becoming like God. The twentieth-century Lutheran theologian Paul Tillich suggested that each great era of church history has a governing image for salvation. In the ancient world, people saw death as the great enemy; in the medieval world it was sin and guilt; in the modern world meaninglessness took center stage. This is not to say that all of these were not involved in salvation, but merely to argue that in each era one of these fundamental issues took prominence. One wonders if in the contemporary postindustrial, post–Cold War, postmodern world the governing image will not be rootlessness and non-belonging. In any case the highest Christian motivation consists in gratitude for God's gift of self in Christ. When thinking about presence below it is crucial to remember that this gift is the gift of a person more than a thing. Grace is a personal self-gift, not a quantity that can be measured. So also it will be necessary to think about Christ's presence in the Eucharist in personal rather than quantitative terms.

To summarize as bluntly as possible: *the ungrateful have no place at the table of the Lord*. In the next section we shall show how the shape of the Eucharist itself plays out this reciprocal dynamic of the gift.

The Eucharist as *Anamnesis* or Memorial of Christ

When considering the accounts of the institution of the Eucharist in chapter 2, especially the accounts of Paul and Luke, we noted that the Greek word *anamnesis* (for the Hebrew *zikkaron*) has a rich meaning. *Anamnesis* signifies more than a psychological remembrance or recalling—it is even more powerful than what modern psychology means by the power of memory. It is a way of speaking about presence and identity. As BEM puts it: "The biblical idea of memorial as applied to the eucharist refers to this present efficacy of God's work when it is celebrated by God's people in a liturgy."[10] Official Catholic documents make the same point when they refer to the "today" of the liturgy. In the power of the Holy Spirit (the focus of the next section) we do far more than say: "Isn't it wonderful that God did those mighty deeds for us in Christ two thousand years ago." Instead we recognize that those acts of God are realized in the present moment and pull us toward God's future. Echoing St. Thomas Aquinas,[11] a beautiful antiphon puts it:

O sacrum convivium in quo Christus sumitur; recolitur
passionis ejus; mens impletur gratia; et futurae gloriae
nobis pignus datur.

(O sacred banquet in which Christ is received; his
passion is recalled; the mind is filled with grace; and a
pledge of future glory given to us.)

The eucharistic banquet brings together past, present and
future in a special way that enables Christ's ecclesial body to
claim its past, be empowered here and now by the activity of
Christ and look forward to God's ultimate vision for the
world. What is remembered is not the Last Supper as such but
the whole of Christ's saving work. Christian prayer always has
its center in Christ. This focus has its own irony since focusing on Christ is focusing on the one who empties himself on
our behalf. So the kenotic or self-emptying one is the center
of our faith and prayer.

Recall that I promised above to lay out a "ritual action" theory of the Eucharist—one centered on the notion of eucharistic
sacrifice. Recall also that the Church from a very early period settled on a pattern of celebrating the Eucharist that telescoped
the actions of the Lord Jesus at the Last Supper:

- Take   Preparation of the Gifts
- Bless   Eucharistic Prayer
- Break   Fraction
- Give   Communion

The four aspects of the properly eucharistic part of the
Mass fit very well with the four-action shape of the Eucharist.
I think they also show that the Church discerned in these same
four actions a way of symbolizing and ritualizing the identity
and action of Jesus. Just as Jesus received his creaturehood

completely—just as he was thoroughly and completely human in the creaturely way that God meant humans to be and not the way that Adam and Eve were when they succumbed to the temptation to become God in their own way—so the preparation of the gifts expresses in a ritual way the acceptance of what God has given. Moreover, Jesus completely acknowledged the Father (the One he called Abba) with every fiber of his being; his whole life and being was a blessing of God. So also the eucharistic prayer blesses God particularly for what has been accomplished in Jesus. Jesus allowed himself to be broken so that his act might become a source of life for those who believe; he was broken and poured out for the life of the world. So also in the fraction and Holy Communion his brokenness his shared by us as the source of life.

It is in this ritual action that the identity (divine and human) of the Lord is made present because his self-gift ("sacrifice" in an ironic sense of the word) is played out. In the mystery of the Incarnation the humanity of Jesus freely responds to his own divine nature. The point of it all is (always with the proviso of the next element: the activity of the Holy Spirit) we too enter into the identity of Christ by playing out his ritual fate. To the extent that we accept our creatureliness and bless God with our lips and our lives, and to the extent that we allow ourselves to be broken and shared with others, to that extent we participate in the presence and sacrifice of the Lord. Of course, Christ's sacramental presence and sacrificial activity are always offered to us in the proper celebration of the Church's Eucharist. But they do not make much sense and are not truly effective unless we receive them with faith and with a readiness to put their implications into action. Thus, to quote Robert Hovda once again, "every liturgy is a peace liturgy" or to repeat the wonderful words of St. Augustine, "Be what you receive."

A "ritual action" theory of the Eucharist proposes that it is precisely on the basis of the eucharistic *activity* of Christ (the sacramental representation of his sacrifice) that we can speak of his presence. In other words, we do not begin with Christ being made present in the bread and wine and then move to thinking about what that presence does. No, in a way that is truer to a more personalist approach to reality and indeed to the liturgy's own basic theology, we move from his activity to his presence and identity. The same process was true of the early Church's itinerary of belief, the one that is recapitulated in every believer: the Lord's divinity (the fact that he is the Incarnate Word, truly divine and truly human) is revealed first and foremost in the cross and resurrection (Paschal Mystery) and only then is it recognized in his origins and his ministry. Interestingly enough, the Catechism takes the same approach by treating the eucharistic presence only after it has dealt with eucharistic sacrifice.[12] In other words, a good theology ends up with Christmas but starts with Good Friday and Easter.

Our earthly gifts of bread and wine are fundamental to this equation since Christian faith, properly understood, is extremely materialistic. To go back to the theology and spirituality of the *berakah,* we can note the fundamental goodness of created things and God's intention that they lead us back to God. At the heart of the Catholic sacramental vision is the affirmation that it is precisely through the material of creation that God saves us—through flesh and blood, through water and oil, through human touch. Too much Christian spirituality has depended on an avoidance of—or flight from—the material world rather than a spiritual engagement with it. Schillebeeckx has it right: *extra mundum nulla salus*—"outside the world there is no salvation." More on this when we come to the fourth section on the communion of the faithful.

This theory is an attempt first of all to affirm the Church's traditional teaching about the Eucharist as a sacrifice. As the BEM notes, the recovery of the biblical notion of memorial or *anamnesis* has been a crucial element in enabling both Protestant and Catholic theologians to see beyond the divisive and polemical issues that split the churches at the time of the Reformation in the sixteenth century. It also affirms that the sacrifice of Christ on the Cross cannot be repeated.[13] The Catechism repeats the same teaching (in line with the Council of Trent) when it insists that the Eucharist *re-presents* the sacrifice of the Cross.[14] Therefore the Mass is not a new sacrifice but rather a participation in the one sacrifice made new and, to use what might seem like somewhat outmoded terminology, whose fruits are applied in the present. This is a way of speaking about the effect of the ritual action of the Eucharist in making Christ's saving activity real for us and for those we love (see box 10.1 on Mass intentions below). The Catechism quotes an ancient prayer of the Church to this effect: "The work of our redemption is carried out as often as the commemoration of this sacrifice is celebrated."[15]

For Catholic teaching the Mass is the sacrifice of the whole Church in which the Church itself is offered in union with Christ's perpetual intercession on behalf of humankind. The Catechism goes on to quote a beautiful passage from St. Augustine's *City of God* that is too good not to repeat here:

> This wholly redeemed city, the assembly and society of the saints, is offered to God as a universal sacrifice by the high priest who in the form of a slave went so far as to offer himself for us in his Passion, to make us the Body of so great a head. . . . Such is the sacrifice of Christians: "We who are many are one Body in Christ." The Church continues to reproduce this sacrifice in the sacrament of the

> altar so well known to believers wherein it is evident to
> them that in what she offers she herself is offered.[16]

It is very important to keep reminding ourselves that sacrifice must be understood paradoxically and ironically as a kind
of antisacrifice. The Mass is not appeasement of an angry God
but rather putting God's saving act for humankind into effect
by accepting his invitation to enter into that very same act.
This kind of (unbloody) sacrifice cannot take place without
our gratefully acknowledging what God has done in Christ.
Therefore sacrifice, *anamnesis* and thanksgiving are all intimately related.

Likewise we recognize that the role of the priest should
be understood with the same kind of paradoxical and ironic
interpretation. After all, Jesus Christ is a very strange kind of
priest in the sense that he did not come from a hereditary
priestly family and did not sacrifice something other than himself but rather emptied himself freely. Ordained priests of the
New Covenant, therefore, are priests in the same way that
Christ is—an ironic way. On behalf of the corporate baptized
priesthood of the faithful, the Church deputes them and
Christ empowers them to stand in Christ's place at a crucial
moment. Why? Because in no other way can the radicality of
God's gift as gift be expressed. Priests do not act on their own
power or commission. The Catechism makes Catholic doctrine on this clear when it agrees with the Fathers of the early
Church (quoting St. John Chrysostom and St. Ambrose) in
affirming that the sacrament comes about by the efficacy of
Christ's word and the action of the Holy Spirit.[17]

From time to time one still hears the rather bizarre question about what would happen if a renegade or unstable priest
went into a bakery and "said the words of consecration." The
only possible answer is, Nothing. The narrative of institution

is not some kind of magical or alchemical formula that turns one thing into another, but rather the prayer of the Church expressed in the words of Christ himself. The priest has only the power to do what the Church intends in its sacramental prayer—nothing more or less. But in the context of the Church's faith the priest is empowered to represent Christ to the Church and the Church to God. A recent decision by the Vatican (mentioned above in chapter 8) to recognize the validity of the ancient Anaphora of Addai and Mari, which does not contain an institution narrative as such, demonstrates that the consecration is more a matter of prayer than it is a matter of a formula of words.

What about real presence and the doctrine of transubstantiation? I suggested earlier that it is better to start with the notion of eucharistic sacrifice and then move to real presence than to start with real presence and then talk about eucharistic sacrifice. In other words, because Christ is active in the liturgy he is present—in a manifold way (the Word proclaimed, the ordained minister, the assembly)—but especially and most concretely in the consecrated bread and wine where, as the Council of Trent affirms in its decree on real presence, "the whole Christ is truly, really, and substantially contained."[18] From the very beginning faithful Christians have confessed the real presence of the Lord and the conversion of the gifts into the Body and Blood of Christ. As I suggest earlier it takes the Catholic sacramental imagination to be able to appreciate how God can be communicated through the material media of this world. (By Catholic sacramental imagination I do not mean to exclude Protestants—and certainly not Orthodox—here, but merely to say that a sacramental vision of creation is one of Catholicism's most precious and characteristic insights.) The term *transubstantiation* which was coined in the twelfth century, first used doctrinally at

Lateran Council IV (1215) and repeated at the Council of
Trent, has often stood as a stumbling block. This is unfortunate because often people who either attack or affirm this
term do not take the trouble to read its most coherent exposition in St. Thomas Aquinas' great textbook, the *Summa
Theologiae*.[19] There St. Thomas makes it abundantly clear that
transubstantiation is not a term that has to do with *physics* but
with *meta*physics. Metaphysics is the philosophical study that
deals with the nature of Being or reality. It's what you study
to get at the root of physics. The substance that transubstantiation is talking about is not what we would normally call a
substance—as in saying that water is a substance. In meta-
physical terms substance means what lies underneath (sub-
stantia) appearances.

So the word *transubstantiation* was coined to enable theologians to steer a narrow course between denial of the real
presence on the one hand and a crude physicalism whereby
Christ's bones would be broken anew and his flesh torn apart
on the other. In other words it's not as if we could figure out
the composition of the consecrated bread and wine if we only
had a sufficiently sophisticated form of chemical analysis. How
can it be that what we see, eat and drink looks like, tastes like
bread and wine? Because its appearances (in technical terms
its "accidents") do not change but its underlying reality (substance) does—such that it isn't even appropriate to think of
these elements as bread and wine. Transubstantiation is not
so much an explanation of this transformation—as if words
could *explain* a miracle of faith—as it is a way of speaking what
Catholic teaching calls "apt." I hope that the "ritual action"
theory of the Eucharist makes the reason for this transformation more plausible in light of our transformation into the
Body of Christ. We need to note one more thing about transubstantiation. St. Thomas makes it clear that "the Body of

Christ is not in the sacrament as in a place." The real presence of Christ is not one of dimensions and weight but rather the presence of a person—human and divine.

But understanding a term properly is one thing and reverencing the mystery of Christ's presence in the Eucharist is quite another. The term describes a way of thinking and talking about eucharistic real presence but it cannot substitute for faith. Ultimately faith in the Eucharist must also involve faith in God's action in the sacrament—the subject of the next section.

But before we proceed we need to tarry just a bit with the notion of presence. It should be clear from what has been said above that the kind of presence we are talking about is the presence of a person, not a thing. We saw in our study of the Eucharist in the New Testament that Christ's words at the Last Supper conveyed his *self-gift*, not the gift of some*thing*. Therefore, the gift of the Eucharist whether received in Holy Communion or adored in prayer before the reserved sacrament is always the gift of Christ beckoning us to respond with our own self-gift. The U.S. United Methodists have expressed this notion beautifully in their anamnesis (memorial) formula, which follows the institution narrative and leads into the memorial acclamation:

> And so, in remembrance of these your mighty acts in
>   Jesus Christ
> we offer ourselves in praise and thanksgiving
> as a holy and living sacrifice,
> in union with Christ's offering for us
> as we say (sing) . . .

When we offer the gifts at the oblation of the Mass, we are being joined by Christ to his own self-offering. The only gift we can really offer is Christ himself, who is transforming not only bread and wine but all of us as the Body of Christ for the salvation of the world.

The Eucharist as Invocation of the Holy Spirit

The eucharistic prayers that we now use show the importance of the role of the Holy Spirit. Although the Roman Canon (Eucharistic Prayer I) does not contain an explicit request that the Father send the Holy Spirit upon the gifts and upon the assembly it does clearly express the notion (and more than once) that eucharistic consecration is the work of God's power and not our own. This is the function of the *epiclesis*, which, as we saw when we considered the eucharistic prayer, always introduces the petition aspect of our praying in the dynamic of proclamation/petition. For centuries Eastern and Western Christians debated whether it was the institution narrative or the invocation of the Holy Spirit that brought about the transformation of the gifts into the Body and Blood of the Lord. No satisfactory answer was ever really found because the question itself was badly put. As the Catechism makes clear, both the "Word of Christ and the action of the Holy Spirit" are required for eucharistic consecration. And, as we saw above, these take place within the context of the Church's prayer proclaimed by the ordained minister.

One of the significant gifts of the BEM statement is that it also emphasizes the Trinitarian dimension of the Eucharist:

> The presence of Christ is clearly the centre of the eucharist, and the promise contained in the words of institution is therefore fundamental to the celebration. Yet it is the Father who is the primary origin and final fulfilment of the eucharistic event. The incarnate Son of God by whom and in whom it is accomplished is its living centre. The

Holy Spirit is the immeasurable strength of love which makes it possible and continues to make it effective. The bond between the eucharistic celebration and the mystery of the Triune God reveals the role of the Holy Spirit as that of the One who makes the historical words of Jesus present and alive.[20]

And so a dimension of sacramental theology that had been in the background for centuries now comes to the forefront. The work of the Holy Spirit makes the Church alive in the power of the Triune God and makes the eucharistic presence a reality. The Church has always relied not only on its commission from the Lord Jesus but also on the constant inspiration and empowerment of the Holy Spirit. The Holy Spirit makes it possible for us to be conformed (configured is the word often favored in official Catholic documents) to the living Christ who gives himself up for the life of the world.

The Eucharist as Communion of the Faithful

One of the most valuable aspects of the renewal of eucharistic theology has been reflection on the meal character of the Eucharist. In the introductory chapter of this book we saw why it makes so much sense to link the meal itself with the fundamental problematic of human existence. To eat and drink is to survive and to share what one eats and drinks is to survive in a manner fitting to the redeemed sons and daughters of God. At times some have written as if there were a conflict between appreciating the Eucharist as meal and as sacrifice. I hope that by this point we can see that no such conflict exists. When understood in the framework of self-gift we can see that the meal is a perfect expression of sacrifice.

BOX 10.2. I WOULD LIKE TO
HAVE A MASS SAID . . .

We have not yet touched on an important aspect of eucharistic theology and piety: the question of Mass intentions. What precisely does it mean to say, "I'd like to have a Mass said for my Aunt Elizabeth, who died."

The desire to associate one's beloved dead with the eucharistic sacrifice is ancient—certainly going back to the third century. The Catechism quotes the beautiful words of St. Monica to her son Augustine: "Put this body anywhere! Don't trouble yourselves about it! I simply ask you to remember me at the Lord's altar wherever you are" (*Confessions* 9.11). And since the fourth century the eucharistic prayers have always contained prayers for both the living and the dead. The practice of the prayers of the faithful also shows that Christians have been concerned to bring their deepest desires and the needs of the world into contact with their most sacred exercise: the eucharistic liturgy.

What then of the idea of a particular or special intention for the Mass? When the young women who lived on the floor of a college dormitory where I was in residence asked to have the mother of one of their classmates remembered at Mass, it made all the sense in the world for us to gather to celebrate the Eucharist praying for the departed and her family. This is a fine and consistent Catholic instinct throughout the ages. But the idea that one should make a monetary offering for a number of

Masses to be said for the deceased is somewhat more difficult to understand especially in light of the recovery of the prayer of the faithful. In order to avoid any sense of "payment" for a sacrament the 1983 Code of Canon Law (no. 945ff.) changes the terminology from "stipend" to "offering." No one can pay for a Mass, but one can make an offering for the support of the Church and expect (legally) that the priest will offer the Mass for the intention of the donor. Since this comes so dangerously close to splitting hairs and since most people seem to have the impression that they are paying for the Mass it would be better to abandon the connection between money and the Eucharist altogether and find some other just way to support the Church and remunerate the clergy. Perhaps books for Mass intentions could be provided in parish churches or a Mass on the anniversary of someone's death announced in the parish bulletin. It is very important that we continue to bring before the Lord those who are dearest to us, both the living and the dead, but it is equally important that we avoid giving the impression that anyone can somehow "buy" salvation. The desire to pray for both the living and the dead is a sign of how important the prayer of the faithful has become.

At the same time we should remember that asking for a special remembrance of a loved one every year—for example on the anniversary of his or her death—is a very praiseworthy practice. As a priest, I have often been extremely moved by families who come to a weekday liturgy in order to remember their beloved dead in this most Christian way.

Some have also questioned whether the Eucharist ought not to be celebrated in the midst of a full meal. Presumably, at least among early Jewish Christians, the blessings that corresponded to Jesus' prayer and words at the Last Supper did frame a meal. Interestingly enough, we have no solid evidence whatsoever of a Christian Eucharist that followed this pattern. On the contrary, our earliest literary evidence from St. Paul seems to argue against having a meal since some are going hungry and thirsty while others are having their fill. Perhaps the apparent meagerness of the Christian meal is another example of irony. God gives us this superabundant bread just as the manna in the desert was given—without excess. (See Exodus 16:13–36.) Only someone with faith could possibly call what we share in the Eucharist a banquet. Moreover, Gordon Lathrop has suggested that the symbolism of only a little food and drink is quite pointed—we need to give the rest away. It is only in the *breaking* of the bread and the *pouring* of the wine that we are enabled to receive divine life. What we have as Christians is never something we can keep as a possession but rather needs to be shared in order to be enjoyed.

It has been said that the Church makes the Eucharist, but the Catechism adds the important truth that "the Eucharist makes the Church."[21] Earlier I suggested that the Eucharist is the ongoing and repeatable sacrament of initiation. In the same paragraph just cited the Catechism states that our communion strengthens the Body of Christ and deepens our incorporation into it. So it is possible to say that the Eucharist itself and the intimate fellowship of the baptized who share at the table is a starting point for a theology of the Church. *Lex orandi/lex credendi*: practice is the foundation of theory. It is not so much that we have a Church with divinely instituted structures that establishes the sacraments as the sacramental experience of Christians that makes a Church possible in the first place. Since there is no genuine sacrament without the foundation of the Word of God (Scripture), we can say that Word and Sacrament are at the root of any good theology of the Church. The Eucharist makes the Church.

The implications of the Communion of the faithful are profound indeed. As we saw in chapter 9, we cannot speak of Communion with the Lord without at the same time speaking of communion with one another. This point is brought home even more starkly by the exchange of peace. How can I not recognize my duty in charity to my brother and sister with whom I exchange a greeting of peace? And how can I limit the implications of that exchange to those that I greet verbally and physically? The Catechism emphasizes the fact that Communion commits us to the poor when it cites a powerful passage from a sermon by St. John Chrysostom:

> You have tasted the Blood of the Lord, yet you do not recognize your brother. . . . You dishonor this table when you do not judge worthy of sharing your food someone judged worthy to take part in this meal. . . . God freed you from all your sins and invited you here, but you have not become more merciful.[22]

In the same vein Pope John Paul II cites another sermon of St. John Chrysostom in his beautiful apostolic exhortation on the celebration of Sunday:

> Do you wish to honor the body of Christ? Do not ignore him when he is naked. Do not pay him homage in the temple clad in silk only then to neglect him outside where he suffers cold and nakedness. He who said: "This is my body," is the same One who said: "You saw me hungry and you gave me no food," and "Whatever you did to the

least of my brothers you did also to me." . . . What good
is it if the eucharistic table is overloaded with golden chalices, when he is dying of hunger? Start by satisfying his
hunger, and then with what is left you may adorn the altar
as well.[23]

We noted above in the section on Eucharist as thanksgiving to the Father that receiving the gift of Christ's person
broken and poured out for us implies no less than our own
self-gift. Practically speaking, this means doing the works of
justice and recognizing the face of Christ in those with whom
I share his Body and Blood—and indeed with all human
beings, for they are represented in my brothers and sisters in
faith. The BEM puts it this way:

> The eucharistic celebration demands reconciliation and
> sharing among all those regarded as brothers and sisters
> in the one family of God and is a constant challenge in the
> search for appropriate relationships in social, economic and
> political life (Matt. 5:23f; I Cor. 10:16f; I Cor. 11:20-22;
> Gal. 3:28). All kinds of injustice, racism, separation and
> lack of freedom are radically challenged when we share in
> the body and blood of Christ. . . . As participants in the
> eucharist, therefore, we prove inconsistent if we are not
> actively participating in the ongoing restoration of the
> world's situation and the human condition.[24]

The very meaning of the Mass is betrayed when we fail
to put its implications into practice by working actively for a
more just world. Faith in the Eucharist means not just verbal
and intellectual belief in doctrines but the response of the
whole person to God's inviting love. The doctrines of Christian
faith are self-implicating: they commit us to action. Thus again

we can see the wisdom of Louis-Marie Chauvet's tripod on which Christian existence rests: Scripture, Sacrament and Ethics. None of these three can ultimately make sense of the Christian life without the other two. And for anyone who desires to be a Christian, the Sacrament of the Eucharist is the necessary bridge between Scripture and Ethics. It literally makes us put our bodies where our mouths are. When Justin Martyr described the collection taken up at the Sunday Eucharist in the second century, he was not describing some-thing that happened *in addition to* the liturgy but rather the profound implications of the liturgy itself.

What about the act of receiving Holy Communion? In my opinion this is an area of the Mass that needs a good deal of reflection today. Those who remember the Mass before Vatican II can recall that we approached the Communion rail of the church and knelt while the priest (or priests) came along the line of kneeling communicants and placed the host on our tongues. The altar server held a plate under our chins lest the slightest fragment fall to the ground. Today we approach Communion stations standing and receive the Body of Christ in our hands or on our tongues and then (at least in many parishes on Sundays) are invited to receive the precious Blood as well. In recent years efforts have been made to ensure that this process happens more reverently. Perhaps we need to reflect more profoundly and more often on the fact that we are not coming forward to receive some*thing*, not even something very holy. We are coming forward to encounter and receive the Son of God who has given himself to us by his dying and rising and continues to give himself to us in this act, which is every bit as intimate as any act we can think of. At times, of course, we can take even the people we love the most deeply for granted and this can happen with our encounter with the Risen Lord in Holy Communion as well.

I remember not long ago seeing the face of an elderly woman who had just received Communion from her newly ordained son. Needless to say, she was beaming. Wouldn't it be wonderful if every encounter with the Risen Lord Jesus in Communion were an experience of the same intensity? Perhaps we need frequent reminders of how awesome this encounter is, and who it is who comes to join us to himself. On the other hand every encounter with someone we love is not earthshaking. Sometimes what is most remarkable is our fidelity to our relationship even when we do not find it exciting. I often like to make the comparison between liturgy and research. When I am doing research, many days are seemingly unproductive and certainly unexciting. They involve the routine of sitting at my desk and taking notes or plowing through material. But every now and again an insight comes or a new way of seeing the material or just a burst of energy. I don't think that those moments happen without the routine of the other less exciting days. They are a gift to be sure—but they are also related to my persistence in doing the work. The same, it seems to me, can be true of personal prayer and public liturgy. Every occasion is not likely to be exciting—but there are glorious moments when our fidelity pays off. Like our experience of human love, Holy Communion involves both ordinary fidelity and experiences of astounding grace.

The Eucharist as Meal of the Kingdom

The profoundly ethical dimension and practical implications of celebrating the Eucharist lead naturally to the fifth of the BEM's categories for describing the meaning of the Eucharist: meal of the kingdom. Every time we celebrate the Eucharist we participate in the already/not yet of Christian salvation. In a very real sense the end of the world has already come in the person of Jesus Christ. He is the world's goal, the perfect image of the unseen God (Colossians 1:15) and the perfect realization of humanity, the Second Adam (Romans 5:12–17). In Christ we perceive what God wants the world to look like in perfect love, freedom and self-gift. And so in the Mass we celebrate what has already been accomplished in Christ. At the same time this end of the world has obviously not yet reached its fulfillment. We look forward to the perfect fulfillment of God's reign of peace and love. And the Eucharist is a foretaste of that heavenly banquet. (The banquet is a much more evocative image of heaven than the beatific vision. It also has the advantage of suggesting the Eucharist.)

One of the earliest eucharistic acclamations we know of comes from the *Didache*, an early-second-century handbook of Christian practice. The phrase is *Maranatha*, which can be translated either "Come, Lord Jesus" or "The Lord Jesus comes."[25] The current Roman Catholic eucharistic prayers themselves beautifully express this same idea. For example, the Eucharistic Prayer for Reconciliation II has at the end of its intercessions:

> Lord,
> as you have welcomed us here to the table of your Son
> in fellowship with Mary, the virgin Mother of God,
> and all the saints,
> so gather at the one eternal banquet
> people of every race, nation, and tongue,
> in that new world
> where the fullness of peace will reign . . .

The Eucharist is an expression of an intense desire for the coming of God's reign and at the same time implies a

commitment to cooperate with the Lord's work in bringing
that reign about. In this context the Catechism refers to St.
Ignatius of Antioch's memorable phrase "the medicine of
immortality, the antidote for death and the food that makes
us live forever in Jesus Christ."[26] Surely we once again find
ourselves in the realm of metaphor, but what a rich metaphor
for the overcoming of the deep wound of selfishness and
grasping in the human condition. The heart of this book's
interpretation of the Mass has been the argument that Christ
is the great reversal of the deep wound in the human condition we call sin and original sin. Further, the eucharistic celebration is the sacramental representation of this work and
personal presence of Christ.

In its treatment of this end-time or eschatological dimension of the Eucharist the BEM focuses on the image of reconciliation that is meant to shine forth in our celebration:

> Reconciled in the eucharist, the members of the body of
> Christ are called to be servants of reconciliation among
> men and women of the joy of the resurrection.[27]

Joy is a fitting concept for us to meditate on as we conclude this reflection on the meaning of the Mass. My student
friend who expressed some skepticism about Mass as sacrifice
was not completely off the mark when he suggested that I
concentrate on celebration. It was just that he presumed the
two ideas to be incompatible. But it seems to me that it is precisely in the revelation of Jesus as the true and trustworthy
source of life in his outpouring of self that constitutes both
eucharistic sacrifice and the source of true Christian joy. Our
celebrations do need to be marked by the joy that comes from
our profound conviction that "God is working his purpose

out," to borrow a phrase from a modern hymn. By joy I do not mean the frozen smile or superficial giddiness that sometimes passes (or tries to pass) for happiness, but rather a deep-down conviction that comes from faith in the fact that God in Christ has already conquered sin and death and that in a mysterious way (and sometimes extraordinarily opaque way) the history of the world and our personal destinies are the working out of that salvation. That is a source and motivation for true happiness indeed. As I mention above in dealing with the meal or communion aspect of the Eucharist, our encounter with Jesus Christ can be an occasion of intense and profound joy—the One who is the world's destiny gives himself to me in the most personal way possible.

The Eucharist is the sharing of that food and drink of the new age where Christ will be all in all and where every tear will be wiped away. For us as Christians this celebration can be a profoundly countercultural experience that questions and criticizes the kinds of social and economic divisions that the world can find so dear to its heart. The royal priesthood of the baptized that God calls into being in Christ is a realm of utter selflessness and profound equality. That is what makes the Eucharist a rich feast, a sumptuous banquet.

The twentieth-century British composer Gerald Finzi wrote an anthem just after the conclusion of World War II entitled "Lo, the Full Final Sacrifice." The anthem took its text from the Roman Catholic priest poet Richard Crashaw's translation of two different texts by St. Thomas on the Eucharist: *Adoro Te Devote* and *Lauda Sion, Salvatorem*. Several lines from the poems provide a wonderful and evocative picture of the power of the Mass to shape our lives as Christians and so a fitting conclusion to this reflection on the meaning of the Eucharist:

O dear Memorial of that Death
Which lives still and allows us breath!
Rich royal food, Bountiful Bread,
whose use denies us to the dead.
Live ever, Bread of loves, and be
My life, my soul, my surer self to me.

Questions for Reflection

1. How does the eucharistic meal mirror the actions of Jesus at the Last Supper?
2. What is Trinitarian about our celebration of the Eucharist?
3. What does the phrase "eucharistic sacrifice" refer to?
4. What do we mean when we talk about transubstantiation?
5. How are Eucharist and social justice related?

Conclusion

In his recent and intensely personal encyclical on the Eucharist, *Ecclesia de Eucharistia*, Pope John Paul II takes some time to reminisce about the many places in the world where he has celebrated the Eucharist: the Cenacle (or Upper Room) in Jerusalem, his parish church in Poland, chapels on mountain paths, lakeshores and seacoasts, sports stadiums and city squares.[1] Obviously this liturgical encounter with Christ has been a most significant aspect of the pope's life. But I hope that we have reflected in the course of this book on those moments of participation in the Mass that have moved us and shown us how Christ is and can be the center of our own lives. I'd like to take the first part of this conclusion to reflect somewhat personally on what I find moving when I attend Mass or when I preside at the liturgy. For the most part I focus on attending Sunday Mass, since that will be the experience of most readers of this book. What makes

the Mass work? Then we shall revisit the question that began
chapter 1: Why bother?

Let's begin with the environment for the celebration. Do
I feel welcome here? I don't need to be smothered when I
walk into a church but I do want to be able to feel that this is
a welcoming place, that the people come here because they
want to be here, that even if I am a stranger I belong here
somehow. Several factors make this possible. There are people at the church doors to welcome me, to hand out whatever
printed materials we'll be needing for the liturgy. (Many
parishes wait until the end of Mass to hand out the bulletin.
I must admit it's extremely disconcerting to see someone
reading the bulletin while I'm preaching, but then again that
might be a good test of whether I am communicating.) Is the
church prepared for the celebration? Are the people reverent
and prayerful? At the same time can I sense that they know
something important is about to happen? In other words, is
Sunday Mass an "occasion" or simply something I have to do,
like grocery shopping? When you walk into a church just
before a wedding you usually get a sense that this is an occasion, that people expect something to happen. Needless to
say, every Sunday is not going to have this same intensity, but
congregations grow in their sense of expectation when they
are in the habit of good liturgical celebration. I can remember walking into St. Peter's Church in downtown Cleveland
a number of years ago. I was immediately taken by people's
sense of expectancy. I was also struck by the care and quality
of the lighting and by the fact that the environment of this
old neo-Gothic church had been transformed to make it a
space for assembly and at the same time very clearly a place
for Catholic liturgy. One thing I look for increasingly when I
enter a liturgical space is a crucifix. Part of what makes a
church Catholic is the tabernacle where the Blessed Sacrament

is reserved. This should be easy to locate and provide a space for personal prayer and adoration. But the primary visual symbol for Christians is the cross of Jesus Christ. I'll admit that I once favored having a cross without a corpus (i.e., not a crucifix) in our churches. This was a bow to the practice of the first Christian millennium, which saw the cross as the sign of both suffering and victory. But the more that I observe Catholics wanting to avoid the suffering Christ, who represents the terrible suffering of the world we live in, the more I realize that having a crucifix may be an antidote to that avoidance. I once visited a well-known "seekers church," where tens of thousands of people gather on Sundays for what could be called good wholesome Christian entertainment rather than divine worship. I asked why there was no cross. The response was that a cross might make people feel uncomfortable. Well, I think that a liturgy that does not recognize our need for both comfort *and* discomfort misses the mark.

How does the liturgy begin? Is the procession orderly without being fussy? Does it have a cross bearer? Someone carrying the Gospel book? Is the accompanying chant or hymn a help to getting into the spirit of worshiping the living God with thankfulness? Does the presider invite us to prayer? Is the penitential rite an opportunity to become conscious of my sinfulness and God's gracious mercy rather than an examination of conscience? Sometimes, particularly at Easter, it is helpful to have the sprinkling with water in place of the usual penitential rite. The sprinkling helps to get in contact—quite physically—with our own baptism. Is the hymn "Glory to God in the Highest" sung? Am I allowed time to pray silently between the presider's invitation "Let us pray" and the collect that sums up our prayer? Affirmative answers to these questions make it likely that this is going to be a very nourishing experience of the Eucharist.

Let's move on to the proclamation of God's word. The first thing I look for here is proclaimers who actually believe what they are reading. I'd rather have someone who believes that this letter of Paul or prophecy from Isaiah or narrative from Genesis expresses the deepest truth of the human condition than listen to the best Hollywood or Broadway performer proclaim something he or she doesn't believe. Of course we want lectors who know how to communicate the spoken word, but their first qualification is Christian faith. Without prejudice to the fact that God is active in the sacraments even when we are not at our best, we can acknowledge that the active faith of those with whom we worship and of those who minister to us has a great effect on our own deepening of faith. Is there a reverent pause after the first reading to let it "soak in"? Is the responsorial psalm sung—at least the response portion? Does the Gospel stand out as a special part of God's word? Is it reverenced with candles and/or incense and the use of a handsome Gospel book?

What about the homily? As a preacher, I hope to interpret God's word in a way that helps my listeners live their lives in a more profoundly Christian way, either by increased understanding of how God is working in our world or by being encouraged to live their faith better. Of course the ideal is both. When I listen to a homily I want the preacher to do the same for me, and I hope that I can hear the Word of God expressed with some imagination, sound theological and biblical background, deep faith and courage. I understand the creed as a wonderful opportunity for us to respond to the Word preached and proclaimed with our own affirmation of faith. As I explain in chapter 4, this response is as much an act of glorifying God as it is an expression of belief. It can easily be sung. In multilingual assemblies I wouldn't hesitate to use the Gregorian chant creed that is familiarly known as

"Credo III." On Easter Sunday the question-and-answer for-
mat of the Apostles' Creed is used with great effect.

When we come to the Prayer of the Faithful, I hope for
intercessions that express our concern and our connection
with the wider Church and world as well as our own needs. I
am also grateful when I am given time to name the names of
people I want to pray for or to voice the intentions I have,
either silently or aloud. This is a moment when we can be in
touch with our great need for God's presence and grace in
our lives and in the life of the world. It need not be rushed.

The presentation of the gifts is a fine moment in the Mass
for me to remember that my whole life is being brought to
the altar with these gifts, that God wants to transform me/us
as well as these gifts of bread and wine. At times a choir will
sing something special at this point, lifting my spirits and
putting me more deeply in touch with the Scriptures and/or
the feast of the day. The eucharistic prayer, too, can be grip-
ping, especially when the preface is sung and when the community joins in heartily in singing the "Holy, Holy" and the
other acclamations. The contemporary liturgy of the Eucharist
is clearly a group effort. It has some of the characteristics of a
ballet or a symphony where many join with their own talents
and roles to make something beautiful and moving. At times
the elevation of the Body and Blood of Christ can be a
moment of great concentration and devotion, not to mention
thanksgiving for the Lord who pours himself out for me.

The Lord's Prayer seems somehow to call for a gesture.
In many communities people stretch out their hands to one
another; in others they lift them up in the traditional gesture
of Christian prayer called the *orans* (praying) position.
Acknowledging this gift that the Lord is giving us, we need
to do something in concert to express our gratitude—and we
need to do it together. The kiss of peace is often a good

opportunity to appreciate the variety of people that God has given to me as partners in worship and to recognize that I cannot be in communion with him if I am not in communion with them. Of course it can also be quite a challenge if I need to exchange the peace with someone who has hurt me or whom I have hurt.

Sacramental Communion with the Lord is very closely connected with my communion with other members of the Body of Christ. I can still remember the first time I attended a Mass at the old Oakland Cathedral (torn down after the earthquake of 1989) and we were invited to stand after receiving Communion until everyone had received. It was one of those "aha!" moments for me. Of course, I said to myself, of course we need to show physically that we are also in communion with one another. And then we sat as the choir sang something beautiful—another way of intensifying our prayer. I admit I feel cheated if I am attending Mass and am not offered the cup. I know intellectually of course that the whole Christ is contained in the consecrated bread, but still the fullness of the sign is missing. And somehow I am making more of a commitment to Communion when I receive from the common cup.

At the conclusion of my best liturgical experiences I feel impelled into the world, impelled to appreciate God's presence in the everyday, impelled to put this great gift I have received into action by the way I deal with others and in my work. Often this is helped by a stirring hymn at the end of Mass. It is also enhanced by communities that want to share some fellowship after the Mass is ended and who linger for some refreshments.

So there you have it—some aspects of my own experience. I hope that you have had similar experiences and that this book will help you to appreciate them more deeply. I should, of course, repeat something I have already said: not every Mass is going to be a great and deeply moving experience, not for the vast majority of us anyway. But there is a great deal to be said for simple fidelity to our worship. St. Ignatius Loyola says in his *Spiritual Exercises* that the person who is experiencing some desolation (dryness, "downness") in prayer can be helped by remembering times of consolation in the past. I think that is true not only of individual prayer but of communal liturgical prayer as well. In any case, the Mass may not always be a deeply emotional experience, but it *is* always an experience of the Lord giving himself to us in his word and his sacramental presence and calling forth our self-giving in return.

Why bother? In chapter 1 the question is, Why bother going to Mass at all when we can worship God anywhere?

1. *Participation in the salvation of the world.* The most important reason for participating in the Eucharist is that God has invited us to share in the experience of the world's salvation in the death and resurrection of the Lord represented every time we celebrate. We are invited to participate in God's redeeming act every time we participate in the Eucharist and thereby commit ourselves to working for God's Reign.

2. *Glory of God—human fully alive—and human alive in Christ.* St. Irenaeus, a second-century Christian theologian and martyr, wrote that the glory of God is the human being fully alive; and that the human being fully alive is the one who is in Christ Jesus. The Mass is where we experience sacramentally our destiny as members incorporated into the Body of Christ. This is what God wants the world to look like—human beings who give of themselves to others in faith, hope and love.

3. *Discipline of faith*. A third reason to bother is the formation of the habit of worshiping and glorifying God. Human beings ordinarily develop by habits, some good and some bad. These are patterns that shape our lives. The discipline of worshiping God helps us to grow into being habitual "adorers of God," even when we don't feel like it.

4. *Hearing the Scriptures communally*. The Bible is the Word of God, but let's face it, individualistic and idiosyncratic readings of the Bible have led to some pretty wacky and even destructive (Jonestown) interpretations. We need to experience the Scriptures both alone and in community. This is what Christians mean by Tradition: the way we have learned throughout history as a Church to interpret the Scriptures together. Hearing the Scriptures in community is a way of deepening as well as safeguarding our experience of God's communication with us.

5. *Developing the moral life*. If I'm right about the basic structure of the Eucharist—taking, blessing, breaking, giving in imitation of the Lord's Passion, death and resurrection—then the habit of weekly (or even more frequent) celebration of the Mass ought to help us in our development as moral human beings. If we celebrate faithfully we ought to be conforming more and more—as individuals and as a community—to the image of generosity and love of the one into whom we were baptized. The final judgment on whether the Mass "works" or not is: "By their fruits shall you know them."

6. *Companionship with Christ*. If I believe that Christ is the Savior of the world, God incarnate, who has given his very self for me, then I want to share in the most inti-

mate experience of self-giving—Holy Communion—
and I also want to recognize him in the brothers and sisters with whom I am sharing the act of self-giving. In
the first chapter we considered our vital human need for
both food and meaning. The word *companionship* is
derived from the Latin *panis* (bread) and *cum* (with).
We find companionship in sharing food with others.
There is no companionship without sharing what our
bodies need. There is no companionship with Christ
except by sharing in his Body—sacrament and Church.

7. *Focusing my needs.* From the earliest days of Christianity
men and women have brought their deepest needs
and desires to the table of the Lord, confident that
they can be joined to Christ's great act of intercession
before the Father (Hebrews 7:25; 10:1–22). This is
why we pray for the dead at Mass; we place them
before the merciful and compassionate God in the
midst of this great work of our redemption. I can
bring all of my deepest desires to the table of the
Lord, confident that I will be heard.

8. *Praying for the world.* Of course we bring not only our
own personal needs but the state of the world to the
celebration of the Eucharist. There is a kind of cosmic
dimension to every celebration in which the realities
of our world (bread, wine, men and women) are
transformed into the Body and Blood of Christ. The
world with all of its needs, joys and struggles is present every time we celebrate the Eucharist together,
and our consciousness of the world helps to make the
Mass the experience of Christian life in a nutshell.

9. *Welcoming the Kingdom.* If the Eucharist is the celebration of how God wants the world to look, then
every time we celebrate, we anticipate the banquet of

God's kingdom "when every tear will be wiped away."[2] In other words, the Reign of God looks like human beings who, frankly recognizing their sinfulness, know that God's mercy is far greater. The Reign of God looks like people who are gathered to receive his Word gratefully. The Reign of God looks like people who allow God's Holy Spirit to form them into a community that accepts life from God, blesses God with everything that is in them, are broken and poured out for other in imitation of the Lord Jesus who has given us this pattern. The Reign of God looks like people who share the most unimaginably precious gifts freely because they know that all is gift in Christ. The Reign of God looks like people who are sent forth to do the works of faith, hope and love with courage.

10. *Pure joy.* A final reason for bothering with the celebration of the Eucharist is that here God invites us to the experience of the deepest peace and joy that is possible— sharing in his own divine life. St. Augustine wrote in his *Confessions*: "O God, you have made us for yourself, and our hearts are restless until they rest in you." The Mass is a foretaste of that perfectly joyful rest. The Mass is an obligation to be sure, but it is an obligation that comes not so much from the outside as from the nature of what it means to enjoy Christian fellowship. We are who we are because of our sharing with our brothers and sisters. And what we share is Jesus Christ himself. How could that not be the cause of pure joy?

The title of this series is Come and See. Nowhere is that invitation from the Lord clearer than in the invitation to share in the celebration of the Mass.

Notes

Chapter 1

1. *Constitution on the Sacred Liturgy,* no. 10.

2. Ernest Becker, *Escape from Evil* (New York: Basic, 1974), 28–29.

3. Margaret Visser, *The Rituals of Dinner* (New York: Penguin, 1991), 17ff.

4. Norman Oliver Brown, *Love's Body* (New York: Vintage, 1966), 167.

5. St. Ignatius of Antioch, Letter to the Ephesians 5:20.

Chapter 3

1. Justin Martyr, *1st Apology* 67, translation taken from *The Ante-Nicene Fathers, vol. 1.*

Chapter 4

1. *General Instruction on the Roman Missal* (2002) no. 46. Hereafter, GIRM.

2. *Constitution on the Sacred Liturgy,* no. 14.

3. See GIRM no. 120. (This exclusion is one of the many relatively minor changes in the third edition of the GIRM.)

4. GIRM no. 48.

5. GIRM no. 47.

6. GIRM nos. 50, 124.

7. GIRM no. 45.

8. GIRM no. 51.

Chapter 5

1. *General Introduction to the Lectionary for Mass* no. 27 (hereafter GILM).

2. GILM no. 3.

3. GIRM no. 59; GILM no. 49.

4. GILM nos. 10, 45; see Liturgy Constitution no. 56.

5. GILM nos. 17, 35–37.

6. GILM no. 32.

7. GILM no. 20.

8. GILM no. 21.

9. GILM no. 28.

10. GILM no. 23.

11. GIRM no. 60.

12. GIRM no. 60; GILM no. 25; Code of Canon Law no. 767:2.

13. GILM no. 24, citing Liturgy Constitution no. 10.

14. GIRM no. 137.

15. GIRM no. 69; emphasis mine.

Chapter 6

1. GILM no. 82.

Chapter 7

1. GIRM no. 72.

2. GIRM no. 72, 5; see also 18–19.

3. GIRM no. 73.

4. GIRM no. 75.

5. GIRM nos. 75, 141.

6. Cyril of Jerusalem, *Mystagogical Catechesis* 5.

7. Tenth Sunday in ordinary time.

8. Twenty-first Sunday in ordinary time.

9. St. Augustine, Sermon 229, translated by Mary Sarah Muldowney, *Saint Augustine: Sermons on the Liturgical Seasons,* The Fathers of the

Church, no. 38 (Washington, D.C.: Catholic University of America Press, 1959), 202.

Chapter 8

1. GIRM no. 78.

2. I am taking the terminology from the work of Italian Jesuit liturgical scholar Cesare Giraudo. Unfortunately, none of Fr. Giraudo's work has been translated into English. See Cesare Giraudo, *Eucaristia per la Chiesa* (Brescia: Morcelliana, 1989).

3. *Directory for Masses with Children,* no. 22.

4. GIRM no. 365.

5. GIRM no. 365.

Chapter 9

1. GIRM no. 80.

2. GIRM no. 85.

3. GIRM no. 81.

4. GIRM no. 83.

5. GIRM nos. 85, 281.

6. GIRM no. 283.

7. GIRM no. 87.

8. GIRM no. 90.

Chapter 10

1. Catechism of the Catholic Church (1994) no. 1322. Hereafter CCC.

2. BEM was viewed as a convergence rather than a consensus statement. Faith and Order requested official responses from all of the member churches, which includes the Roman Catholic Church, a number of Orthodox churches and a great number of Protestant churches. The responses have been collected in six volumes and are themselves a gold mine for ecumenical theology.

3. CCC nos. 1356–81.

4. CCC nos. 1382–1401.

5. CCC nos. 1402–5.

6. See, for example, the fine book by French theologian Louis-Marie Chauvet, *The Sacraments.*

7. St. Augustine, Sermon 227.

8. BEM, Eucharist no. 4.

9. CCC no. 1327.

10. BEM, Eucharist no. 5.

11. St. Thomas Aquinas, *Summa Theologiae* part 3, question 60, article 3. The impact of this wonderful antiphon can be felt in listening to the haunting, gorgeous musical setting by Olivier Messaien, a late-twentieth-century mystical French composer.

12. CCC nos. 1356–81.

13. BEM, Eucharist no. 8.

14. CCC nos. 1362–66.

15. CCC nos. 1363–64; see Prayer over the Gifts, Mass for the Lord's Supper, Holy Thursday in the Sacramentary of Verona.

16. CCC no. 1372, *City of God* 10:6; see Hebrews 7:25–27; CCC nos. 1368–69.

17. CCC no. 1375.

18. CCC no. 1374.

19. St. Thomas Aquinas, *Summa Theologiae*, part 3, question 75.

20. BEM, Eucharist no. 14.

21. CCC no. 1396.

22. St. John Chrysostom, Homily on 1 Corinthians 27:5; CCC no. 1397.

23. St. John Chrysostom, Homily on St. Matthew; Pope John Paul II, *Dies Domini* no. 71.

24. BEM, Eucharist no. 20.

25. *Didache* 10; see CCC no. 1403.

26. St. Ignatius of Antioch, *To the Ephesians* 20.2.

27. BEM, Eucharist no. 24.

Conclusion

1. John Paul II, "On the Eucharist in Its Relationship to the Church," *Ecclesia de Eucharistia,* April 17, 2003 (Vatican City: Libreria Editrice Vaticana, no. 8); see also no. 59.

2. Eucharistic Prayer 3; insertion for funerals.

For Further Study

Adam, Adolf. *The Eucharistic Celebration: The Source and Summit of Faith*. Collegeville, Minn.: Liturgical, 1994.

Alison, James. *The Joy of Being Wrong: Original Sin through Easter Eyes*. New York: Continuum, 1997.

Baldovin, John F. "Eucharistic Prayer." In *The New Westminister Dictionary of Liturgy and Worship*, edited by Paul Bradshaw, 192–99. Knoxville: Westminster John Knox, 2002.

Baldovin, John, ed. *Robert Hovda: The Amen Corner*. Collegeville, Minn.: Liturgical, 1993. "Peace liturgies are the only kind we have."

Baptism, Eucharist, and Ministry. Faith and Order Paper 111. Geneva: World Council of Churches, 1982.

Becker, Ernest. *Escape from Evil*. New York: Basic, 1974.

Bradshaw, Paul. *The Search for the Origins of Christian Worship*. 2d ed., rev. Oxford: Oxford University Press, 2002.

Brown, Norman O. *Love's Body*. New York: Vintage, 1966.

Bugnini, Annibale. *The Reform of the Liturgy, 1948–1975*. Collegeville, Minn.: Liturgical, 1990. See especially chapters 24–25. Archbishop Bugnini can rightfully be called the architect of the Vatican II liturgical reform. See especially chapter 29.

Cabié, Robert. *The Eucharist*. Vol. 2, *The Church at Prayer*. Edited by A. G. Martmort. Collegeville, Minn.: Liturgical, 1986.

The Catechism of the Catholic Church. Rome: Libreria Editrice Vaticana, 1994.

Chauvet, Louis-Marie. *The Sacraments: The Word of God at the Mercy of the Body.* Collegeville, Minn.: Liturgical, 2001.

Chilton, Bruce. *Jesus' Prayer and Jesus' Eucharist: His Personal Practice of Spirituality.* Valley Forge, Pa.: Trinity Press International, 1997.

Chupungco, Anscar, ed. *The Eucharist: Handbook for Liturgical Studies III.* Collegeville, Minn.: Liturgical, 1999. See especially the chapters by Michael Witczak and Jan Michael Joncas.

Crocker, Richard. *An Introduction to Gregorian Chant.* New Haven, Conn.: Yale University Press, 2000.

Crockett, William. *Eucharist: Symbol of Transformation.* Collegeville, Minn.: Liturgical, 1988. A very readable survey of eucharistic theology from an Anglican.

Fitzgerald, Sally, ed. *The Habit of Being: The Letters of Flannery O'Connor.* New York: Vintage, 1980.

Foley, Edward. *From Age to Age: How Christians Have Celebrated the Eucharist.* Chicago: Liturgy Training Publications, 1992.

Girard, René. *I Saw Satan Fall Like Lightning from Heaven.* New York: Orbis, 2001.

Huck, Gabe. *The Communion Rite at Sunday Mass.* Chicago: Liturgy Training Publications, 1994.

Janowiak, Paul. *The Holy Preaching: The Sacramentality of the Word in the Liturgical Assembly.* Collegeville, Minn.: Liturgical, 2000.

John Paul II. *"On Keeping the Lord's Day Holy" (Dies Domini).* Apostolic Exhortation, 1998.

Jungmann, Josef. *Missarum Sollemnia: The Mass of the Roman Rite.* 2 vols. Translated by F. Brunner. New York: Benziger, 1951.

———. *The Liturgy of the Word.* 4th ed. London: Burns & Oates, 1966.

Keifer, Ralph. *To Give Thanks and Praise.* Washington, D.C.: Pastoral, 1980.

———. *To Hear and Proclaim: Introduction to the Lectionary for Mass.* Washington, D.C.: Pastoral, 1983.

Kilmartin, Edward. *The Eucharist in the West: History and Theology.* Collegeville, Minn.: Liturgical, 1998.

Kodell, Jerome. *The Eucharist in the New Testament*. Collegeville, Minn.: Liturgical, 1988.

Lathrop, Gordon. *Holy People: A Liturgical Ecclesiology*. Minneapolis: Fortress, 1999.

———. *Holy Things: A Liturgical Theology*. Minneapolis: Fortress, 1993.

Laverdiere, Eugene. *The Eucharist in the New Testament and the Early Church*. Collegeville, Minn.: Liturgical, 1996.

Leonard, John K., and Nathan Mitchell. *The Posture of the Assembly during the Eucharistic Prayer*. Chicago: Liturgy Training Publications, 1994.

Léon-Dufour, Xavier. *Sharing the Eucharistic Bread: The Witness of the New Testament*. Translated by Matthew J. O'Connell. New York: Paulist, 1982.

Liturgy Training Publications. *Handbook for Lectors and Gospel Readers*. Chicago: Liturgy Training Publications.

———. *Sourcebook for Sundays and Seasons*. Chicago: Liturgy Training Publications. These two almanacs, published yearly, are extremely valuable in preparing the Liturgy of the Word.

Macy, Gary. *The Banquet's Wisdom*. New York: Paulist, 1992. A fine summary of eucharistic theology in the course of Church history.

Marravee, William. *The Popular Guide to the Mass*. Washington, D.C.: Pastoral, 1992.

Mazza, Enrico. *The Celebration of the Eucharist: The Origin of the Rite and the Development of Its Interpretation*. Collegeville, Minn.: Liturgical, 1999.

———. *The Eucharistic Prayers of the Roman Rite*. Collegeville, Minn.: Liturgical, 1986.

McCarron, Richard. *The Eucharistic Prayer at Sunday Mass*. Chicago: Liturgy Training Publications, 1997.

Metzger, Marcel. *History of the Liturgy: The Major Stages*. Collegeville, Minn.: Liturgical, 1997.

Mitchell, Nathan. *Real Presence: The Work of Eucharist*. 2d ed. Chicago: Liturgy Training Publications, 2002.

Murphy-O'Connor, Jerome. "Eucharist and Community in I Corinthians." In *Living Bread, Saving Cup: Reading on the Eucharist*. Edited by R. Kevin Seasoltz. Collegeville, Minn.: Liturgical, 1987.

New Proclamation. Minneapolis: Fortress. This series appears several times each year according to liturgical seasons. It provides commentaries on the readings that take account of the liturgical context.

Nocent, Adrian. *Days of the Lord*. 6 vols. Collegeville, Minn.: Liturgical, 1991.

————. *The Liturgical Year*. 4 vols. Collegeville, Minn.: Liturgical, 1977.

Nodet, Etienne, and Justin Taylor. *The Origins of Christianity*. Collegeville, Minn.: Liturgical, 1998.

Power, David. *The Eucharistic Mystery: Revitalizing the Tradition*. New York: Crossroad, 1992.

Rahner, Karl. "The Theology of the Symbol." In *Theological Investigations IV*, 221–52. Baltimore: Helicon, 1966.

Schillebeeckx, Edward. *Christ: The Sacrament of the Encounter with God*. New York: Sheed & Ward, 1987.

————. *Church: The Human Story of God*. New York: Crossroad, 1990.

Schmemann, Alexander. *The Eucharist: Sacrament of the Kingdom*. Crestwood, N.Y.: St. Vladimir's Seminary Press, 1988. A beautiful commentary in twelve movements by a scholar from the Orthodox Church in America.

Sheerin, Daniel, ed. *The Eucharist (Message of the Fathers of the Church)*. Collegeville, Minn.: Liturgical, 1986. A collection of important passages regarding the Eucharist in the writings of the early Church.

Stone, Darwell. *A History of the Doctrine of the Holy Eucharist*. 2 vols. London: Longman's, Green, 1909.

Taft, Robert. *Beyond East and West: Problems in Liturgical Understanding*. 2d ed., rev. Rome: Pontifical Oriental Institute, 1999.

————. *A History of the Liturgy of St. John Chrysostom: The Precommunion Rites*. Rome: Pontifical Oriental Institute, 2000. Although this work, part of a larger six-volume history, obviously deals with the Byzantine liturgy, Taft surveys many important questions having to do with the Lord's Prayer and the Fraction Rite.

Tillich, Paul. *The Courage to Be*. New Haven, Conn.: Yale University Press, 1952.

Visser, Margaret. *The Rituals of Dinner*. New York: Penguin, 1991.

Wright, N.T. *The Lord and His Prayer*. Grand Rapids, Mich.: Eerdman's, 1997. A commentary on the Our Father.

Index

About the Author

John F. Baldovin, S..J., is professor of historical and liturgical theology at Weston Jesuit School of Theology in Cambridge, Mass. Since 1994 he has worked with the International Commission on English in the Liturgy (ICEL) and has also served as president of the North American Academy of Liturgy and the ecumenical international Societas Liturgica.